The Rescuers

TEN TRUE TALES

The
Rescuers

Kids Who Risked Everything to Save Others

Allan Zullo

SCHOLASTIC INC.

New York   Toronto   London   Auckland   Syndney
Mexico City   New Delhi   Hong Kong   Buenos Aires

ISBN 0-439-85483-0

12 11   12 13 14 15 16/0

Printed in the U.S.A.
First printing, October 2006

Cover photo credits
House on fire © Richard H Johnston/Taxi/Getty Images
Child jumping © Tim O'Leary/zefa/Corbis

To Wyatt and Gabrielle Rancourt, with the
hope they will discover their inner strength
whenever times are tough.
—A.Z.

To learn more about the author,
go to www.allanzullo.com

Contents

Kid Heroes   1

Up in Flames   3

The Flood and the Fury   17

The Edge of Disaster   31

On Thin Ice   44

The Cesspool   58

Dead Man's Bridge   71

The Ball of Fire   82

The Tower of Terror   96

The Desperate Race   110

The White Death   121

KID
HEROES

Real heroes — not the ones on the silver screen or on the playing field — come from all walks of life. Some, such as police officers and firefighters and soldiers, have performed brave acts in the line of duty. Many others are just ordinary folks who, when faced with extraordinary situations, have shown incredible courage to help other people.

But grown-ups don't have a monopoly on heroism. Many kids have voluntarily endangered their own lives in daring efforts to rescue others from deadly circumstances.

In this book you will read ten amazing, life-and-death ordeals of young people who risked everything to save lives. For example, a 13-year-old boy braved raging floodwaters during the height of a killer hurricane to rescue a family of twelve . . . a teenage babysitter repeatedly ran into a blazing house to save the lives of five children . . . a high school athlete spent 17 hours on a frozen ledge in a blizzard to keep an injured avalanche victim alive . . . an eighth grader climbed a 40-foot-tall electrical transmission tower to prevent a mentally challenged child from falling.

These stories are based on, or inspired by, true accounts ripped from the headlines. Although the basic details of the heroic actions are accurate, the dialogue and many scenes have been dramatized, and names and places have been changed to protect everyone's privacy.

These young heroes never gave up. Despite the dire situations and overwhelming obstacles that they encountered, these courageous kids found the inner strength to persevere during dangerous rescues. They did what they believed had to be done, no matter the risk, no matter the cost to their own safety. In every case, it was worth it — because these heroes saved lives.

UP IN FLAMES

Mrs. Emerson seemed uneasy as she went over the final instructions for Sarah Barger. "The little ones — Ellie and Ginny — need to be in bed no later than eight. The older kids can stay up until ten." Mrs. Emerson looked into the 15-year-old babysitter's pale blue eyes and said, "Are you sure you can handle five children?"

Sarah tossed her long blond hair and replied, "Of course. I've been babysitting since I was thirteen. Haven't lost a kid yet."

Mrs. Emerson wasn't amused. "They can be a handful, especially with new sitters. The children are used to having their regular sitter, Miss Norquist. But she was feeling poorly. She recommended you."

"Please don't worry about a thing. I've had first-aid training and I love kids. We'll get along fine."

"They can get a little unruly. In fact, they lost their television privileges because of their misbehavior earlier today."

The kids, who had already kissed their parents good-bye, were in the kitchen eating dessert.

Mr. Emerson, who had been trying to get his wife out the door, finally took her hand and said, "It's time to go." Turning to Sarah, he said, "We'll be home around midnight."

As he led his wife out into the Wisconsin winter night, Mrs. Emerson stopped, turned, and told Sarah, "Make sure you lock the door behind us. Phone numbers on how to reach us, the doctor, and our nearest neighbor are on the kitchen door. And, please, no visitors. That includes your friend Robert."

This town is way too small for me, thought Sarah. *Even a woman I've never met before tonight knows I'm dating Bobby Swanberg.*

"Say 'good night,' dear," Mr. Emerson said, pulling his wife toward the car.

"Good night, Sarah — and don't let the little ones out of your sight."

As the couple walked through the fresh snow toward the driveway, Sarah heard Mr. Emerson tell his wife, "You seem to be fretting more than usual."

"I know. I have a bad feeling about tonight."

Sarah rolled her eyes. *Nothing bad is going to happen,* she told herself. Never in her worst nightmare could she have imagined the terror she would face and the bravery she would need a few hours from then.

The petite high-school sophomore was babysitting for the Emerson children — Ellie, three; Ginny, five; Raymond, seven; and Sally, nine — and Sally's friend Marsha, also nine. The Emersons lived in a turn-of-the-century, two-story farmhouse in the middle of a 200-acre spread about five miles from Janesville. The nearest neighbor was about a half mile away.

After locking the front door, Sarah swung open the kitchen door and let out a yelp. "What are you kids doing?" What they were doing was pouring chocolate syrup over Ellie's head and smearing it on her face.

"Ellie doesn't mind," Raymond said. "She loves chocolate."

The giggling little girl was licking her lips and fingers and nodding.

This is going to be a long, long night, Sarah thought.

After she cleaned up Ellie and the kitchen, Sarah tried to keep the kids entertained. She played board games with them, made shadows on the wall, and had them act out their favorite TV characters. She also mopped up two spilled drinks, removed the bubble gum that Raymond had stuck in Sally's hair, returned the sofa cushions that the two youngest had swiped, and took away the marking pen that the mischievous Raymond was planning to use on the hallway. All this within the first two hours.

This is not going well, Sarah told herself. *I wish I could get Bobby to help me.* Her 16-year-old boyfriend, who lived on a farm a few miles from the Emerson's, had called her earlier in the day. During their chat, Bobby suggested that maybe he would drive by the house later that night when the kids were in bed "just to make sure you're doing all right." *I better call him and tell him he can't come inside*, she told herself. She dialed his number, but the line was busy.

She moved her babysitting operation to the upstairs bed-rooms. With Sarah's blessing, Sally and Marsha began making beaded necklaces from a kit. While Sarah was getting the two youngest ready for bed, Raymond, who was supposed to be in his room playing with his toy trucks, charged into the youngest girls' room.

Wearing a large, red towel as a cape, he announced, "I'm Superman!" He jumped back and forth between Ellie's bed and Ginny's bed before running down the hallway. Then he burst into Sally's bedroom and leaped on her bed, sending hundreds of tiny beads scattering in all directions. Sally and Marsha screamed in anger.

Before they could retaliate, Sarah raced in. Pretending to be the Kryptonite Queen, Sarah rendered Superman's power useless and put him in jail — his bedroom. Meanwhile, she placed a Kryptonite shield in front of Sally's bedroom door, so Superman couldn't enter it without asking Sarah to disable it.

After Raymond settled down, Sarah read *Goodnight Moon* to Ellie and Ginny, then tucked them into bed. Next she went into Raymond's room and told him a story about how Superman saved the day when he deflected the mad scientist's death ray from the city of Metropolis. The boy fell asleep just as she finished her tale.

She peeked into Sarah's room and said, "If you girls keep it down, you can stay up a little later. But, Sally, don't tell your mother."

Sarah went back downstairs and finally had a chance to relax. Her quiet time wouldn't last long.

What she didn't know was that when she was getting the little girls ready for bed, Raymond had sneaked downstairs to the laundry room next to the kitchen. He climbed onto the washing machine to reach the cabinet that contained old towels and rags. When he pulled out the red beach towel to use as his Superman cape, he didn't notice that several rags had fallen to the floor. One of the rags landed against the opening of a space heater that was running to keep the water pipes from freezing overnight.

The rag began smoldering until it caught fire, igniting the other rags and dirty clothes that were on the floor. The small flames crept along the linoleum before reaching the wall. Slowly, the flames grew bigger, and smoke began belching out of the laundry room and into the kitchen.

Sarah, who was in the living room in the front of the house, was reading a book when her nose began to twitch. *Smells like smoke,* she thought. *But the Emersons don't smoke.* She examined the fireplace. The embers were cold and dark. *I'd better check the kitchen.* The moment she opened the kitchen door, she was engulfed in smoke and heat.

She was so surprised that she gasped and inhaled a lungful of smoke, setting off a series of coughs. Hurrying to the phone in the hallway, she picked it up, but the line was dead. Afraid to waste another second, she bounded up the stairs and pounded on the bedroom doors. "Fire!" she shouted. "Fire! Get up! Get up!"

She dashed into the little girls' room and woke them. She scooped up Ellie and dragged Ginny out of bed. "Follow me!" she ordered Ginny. Smoke was billowing in the upstairs hallway. "Raymond!" she yelled. "Fire! Run! Run!"

She opened his door and made sure he was awake. Then she scurried into Sally's room. "Girls! Hurry! Hurry! The house is on fire!" Marsha jumped out of bed and threw on her jeans and sweater. Sally put a sweater over her pajamas. In the hallway, smoke was curling up the walls and ceiling. Assuming everyone was behind her, Sarah, who was still carrying a wailing Ellie, yelled, "Hold your breath and follow me! We're going to make a run for it out the front door!" She scampered down the stairs and darted through the smoke-filled living room. She flung open the front door and ran into the snow until she felt they were a safe distance from the burning house.

"Whew, we made it!" she declared.

But when she and Ellie turned around, Sarah realized that Marsha was the only child who had followed her. "Oh, no! Where are the rest of them?"

"I don't know," Marsha replied. "I thought they were right behind me."

Ellie was shivering from fright and the winter air. Sarah handed her over to Marsha and said, "Take care of her while I go back inside."

Sarah took a step and pulled off her sweater. "Here, Marsha, wrap this around Ellie." Looking directly at the scared little girl, she said, "Everything will be all right, Ellie. I promise. Marsha will take good care of you."

Sarah raced back into the house. Fire had spread into the living room and had reached the bottom of the stairs. "Sally! Raymond! Ginny! Get down here!"

There was no answer. *I can't leave them up there to burn.* She leaped over the flames at the base of the stairs and flew up the steps. In the hallway, she groped through the choking smoke, her hands feeling the wall until she came to Sally's bedroom. Sally was cowering in the corner, too panic-stricken to move.

"Sally, give me your hand. Please. We need to get out of here right now."

In a daze, Sally stood up and squeezed Sarah's hand. With Sally in tow, Sarah went into Raymond's room. The boy was sprawled on the bed. Sarah shook him awake and gave him a gentle slap until he opened his eyes. "Hold on to Sally's hand," she ordered.

Then the three of them headed into Ginny's room. At first, Sarah couldn't find the five-year-old. "Ginny! Ginny! Where are you?" She dropped to her knees and looked under the bed. The little girl was curled up in a ball. Sarah pulled her out. Throwing Ginny over her shoulder, Sarah ordered the other two to hold hands and follow her.

When they reached the top of the stairs, flames were licking at the lower steps and scaling both walls of the stairway. "Get down on your hands and knees and don't move," she ordered the others. "Stay *below* the smoke. I'll be right back."

She dashed into the bathroom, snatched several towels, and soaked them in the sink. Then she hurried back to the kids and wrapped their heads, and hers, in the wet towels. "Okay, we're going to run right through those flames as fast as we can." But by now, the flames were taller than six feet. Holding Ginny in her arms, Sarah charged down the steps and leaped through the flames.

The heat was intense; the smoky air almost unbearable to

breathe. Flames seared her legs and arms as she sprinted through the fire and out the door. "Thank God, we made it!" she shouted, ignoring the burns through her scorched jeans and blouse.

When they reached Marsha and Ellie, Marsha asked, "Where's Sally? Where's Raymond?"

"What?" Sarah whipped around. "Noooo! They were right behind me." She handed Ginny to Marsha. "Here, take Ginny. I've got to find the other two."

"But, Sarah, you can't go in the house now. Look."

Flames were shooting out the front door and all the windows on the first floor. *What if the kids fell on the stairs or didn't make it through the flames? They'll be killed for sure. I've got to find a way to save them.* "I can't let them die in there."

Sarah ran to the side of the house and looked up at the closed window in Sally's room. Although she couldn't see any fire in the room, it was filling up with deadly smoke. Without a ladder, there was no way to reach the second floor.

Suddenly, the window opened and smoke spewed out. Through the blackness, she spotted Sally leaning out as far as she could. Behind Sally, flames had begun to spread into the bedroom.

"What am I going to do?" Sally wailed.

"Jump! Jump!" cried Sarah.

"But I'll kill myself!"

"No you won't. There's a soft evergreen bush and plenty of snow on the ground to break your fall."

"I'm scared."

"I know, Sally, but if you don't jump now, you'll burn to death. Now jump!"

Seating herself on the windowsill, Sally thrust one foot outside and hesitated.

"You can do it!" Sarah said. "Just let go."

Moaning and crying, Sally looked down and then back inside. The flames had reached the window, singeing her hair. She let out a scream, lost her balance, and fell from the window. But her foot got caught in the pull strings of the window shade. She was suspended head down, hanging by her ankle from the window. Adding to her desperation, her pajamas had caught fire. "Help me! Help me! Aah! I'm burning!" Seconds later, Sally managed to squirm free and plunge into the evergreen.

Sarah sprinted over and smothered Sally's burning clothes with snow. After pulling Sally, who was now unconscious, away from the burning house, Sarah gently rubbed snow on Sally's face to revive her.

"My arm hurts real bad," Sally groaned.

"Did you see Raymond?"

"Yes, he was afraid to go down the stairs. I think he ran back to his room."

Sarah looked up at the blazing house. *The flames haven't reached that part of the house yet. Maybe there's still hope. But how am I going to get up there?*

Just then, a pickup truck roared into view. "Bobby!" Sarah shouted.

Bobby jumped out of the truck. "I was coming over to see you and then I saw . . . My God, Sarah, this is terrible. Is everybody safe?"

"Everybody but Raymond. He's in his room up there on the far left. But there's no way to get to him."

"Yes, there is," he said, pointing to the pickup. The vehicle, which belonged to his father, who was a farmer and painting contractor, carried an extension ladder. Bobby lugged it over to the house and raised it until it reached Raymond's window.

"Shouldn't I go up there?" said Sarah. "You know, because of your asthma."

"Not a chance. I'm stronger. I'll be fine. Get the rest of the kids in the truck and turn on the heater. They must be frozen by now."

He scampered up the ladder and tried to open the window, but it was locked. So he whipped off his stocking cap, wrapped it around his fist, and broke the glass. Then he reached in and unlatched the window. Smoke poured out, temporarily blinding him and causing him to cough violently.

"Raymond! Raymond! Are you in there?" he yelled. All he heard was the crackling of the flames. Bobby held his breath and tumbled into the room. "Where are you, Raymond? Where are you?" he shouted, frantically feeling around the bed. Bobby tried to ignore the pain in his lungs and the urge to cough, but he couldn't. He turned back to the window and took a few gulps of air. He reached in his jacket pocket for his inhaler, a device that pushes a medicinal spray into his lungs. *It's not here! It must have fallen out of my pocket.* Within seconds, he suffered a severe coughing fit that dropped him to his knees. But Bobby was determined to make one more rescue attempt.

He knew he had little time left to find Raymond. *If he's in here, he's either under the bed or in the closet,* Bobby thought. *If I'm a little boy, where would I hide? The closet.* Crawling on his belly so he could stay below the sinking level of the smoke, Bobby felt the wall until he reached the closet door.

He opened it and fumbled around in the darkness. "Raymond! Are you in here?" There was no reply. The smoke had sunk almost to the floor. He was out of time. Stretching his arms and wildly feeling the floor, Bobby was ready to give up when he touched a foot. His fingers wrapped around an ankle. *I got him!*

Clasping Raymond's leg, Bobby pulled the unconscious boy to him and felt his chest. *Good. He's alive.* Bobby crawled toward the window, dragging Raymond with him. Feeling like his lungs were being squeezed in a vice, Bobby suffered another violent and painful coughing fit that left him barely able to move. He reached the windowsill and then collapsed.

So close, he thought. *So close.* Suddenly he felt two hands grip his wrists.

"Bobby! You've got to get out of here!" It was Sarah. She had climbed up the ladder to help him.

Still hacking from the smoke he had inhaled, Bobby got to his knees and handed the limp, unconscious boy to Sarah. Unfortunately, because she was so small, she didn't have the strength to carry Raymond, who was slightly overweight, down the ladder.

"Bobby, I need your help."

Although wheezing badly and unable to catch his breath, Bobby stood up. He took off his belt, put it under Raymond's arms, and buckled it. Between his wheezes and coughs, he told Sarah, "Get under Raymond . . . so his legs . . . are on your shoulders . . . I will be . . . above him . . . holding . . . on to the belt . . . Let's go."

To take some of the boy's weight off Sarah's shoulders, Bobby put one hand on the rung of the ladder while the other gripped the belt around Raymond's chest. Slowly they brought him to the ground and lay him in the snow.

Sarah leaned over Raymond. "He's not breathing!"

She remembered her A-B-C checklist that she had learned in first-aid class. *"A" for airway.* Sarah tilted his head back to make sure there was nothing blocking his airway. *It's clear. Go to "B" for breathing.* She pinched his nose with her fingers, covered his mouth with hers, and gave two breaths. *Nothing! Okay, go to C — circulation and compression.* She pressed her fingers against his neck and felt his carotid artery for a pulse. *Still nothing!* She pressed on his chest. *One . . . two . . . three . . . four . . . five . . . Come on, Raymond. Breathe. Breathe!*

She blew another breath into him. Suddenly, she felt him move, then cough and gasp. Sarah slumped to the ground. "Thank goodness."

Raymond was groaning, mumbling, and shivering. His pajamas were singed and covered with soot. She sat Raymond up and held him tight. "You're going to be fine," she cooed. "We're all going to be fine. Isn't that right, Bobby?"

She looked behind her and screamed. Bobby was sprawled on all fours gasping for breath. Exertion, smoke inhalation, and anxiety had combined to give him the worst asthma attack of his life. "Where's your inhaler?" she asked.

"Lost," he rasped. "Fell out . . . of my jacket."

In the glow of the fire, she could see that Bobby's lips and fingers were turning blue. *My God. He's in serious trouble.*

"Sally!" Sarah shouted. "Marsha! Come here!" When they ran over to her, she said, "Take care of Raymond. I've got to find Bobby's inhaler."

Sarah hugged Bobby. "Try to stay calm. I'll find your inhaler."

The aluminum ladder, which was still propped against the window, was melting at the top from the incredibly intense heat. Sarah madly scanned the ground where the snow had melted. *There it is!* The inhaler was lying under the ladder close to the flames. She rubbed her face in snow, hoping to blunt the heat on her skin. Then she counted to three and sprinted as fast as she could toward the burning building. With one swipe, she picked up the inhaler and rushed back to Bobby.

"Here's your inhaler. It's pretty warm but it doesn't look damaged."

He put the inhaler in his mouth and sucked in the medication, which quickly brought his breathing under control.

"You can relax now," she said.

"So . . . can you . . . Sarah."

The volunteer firefighters — alerted by the nearest neighbor — had arrived. But there was little they could do for the house, which by now was nearly consumed by fire. They let the blaze burn out on its own and made sure no flying embers ignited the outbuildings or the nearby field.

Ambulances took the children and the two teenagers to the hospital. Ellie, Ginny, and Marsha had a few scrapes and minor burns on their arms. Sally had broken her right arm. Raymond and Bobby were treated for smoke inhalation. Sarah suffered first- and second-degree burns on her arms and legs.

While they were being treated in the hospital, Bobby told Sarah, "What you did tonight — saving all those lives — was incredibly brave. You're a real-life hero."

"And so are you, Bobby. Raymond would be dead if it hadn't been for you." She leaned her head on her boyfriend's shoulder. "The next time I babysit for someone, I'm going to insist on one condition."

"What is it?"

"That you are allowed to come by the house to check on me anytime you want."

THE FLOOD AND
THE FURY

"Hurricane Katrina is now a category-five storm with wind gusts up to one hundred seventy-five miles an hour — and it's heading directly toward us," the weatherman warned grimly. "It's expected to hit the Biloxi area in the early morning hours tomorrow with devastating force. Widespread flooding and catastrophic damage are expected."

A hush fell over the four adults and nine children who were watching television in the cramped living room of the small A-frame house in one of the poorest neighborhoods in Biloxi, Mississippi. Lying on the floor, 13-year-old Peter Ballard, who was using his yellow Labrador retriever, Duke, as a pillow, put down the superhero comic book he was reading and stared at the TV.

"The storm surge — the onshore rush of seawater caused by Katrina's high winds — could rise as much as twenty to thirty feet," the weatherman said. "Officials urge everyone living in low-lying areas to evacuate immediately."

Peter and the others in the house — all relatives of his — planned to ride out the storm together here in the home of his grandmother, Lenore Pitts. Seeing the worried look on the faces of the others in the room, Peter declared, "I'm not worried, Grandma. I think this is going to be just like Hurricane Ivan — no big deal."

Ivan had slammed into the area the year before, in 2004. Forecasters had predicted that it would cause considerable destruction in his hometown, but the hurricane packed less of a punch than predicted, and Biloxi escaped major damage.

"I agree with you, Peter," Grandma said. "I'm staying right here."

Outside in the darkness, the howling wind and pelting rain lashed against the windows and pounded the tin roof, making it hard to hear the TV weatherman. Peter ignored him and returned to his stack of comic books to pass the time.

Across the room, his twin sister, Prissy, was nervously twisting her braided hair. "Why is it that all the bad storms come at night?" she whimpered. "It's scary."

"There's nothing to be afraid of," Peter said. "It will be over by morning."

The room was hot, sticky, and crowded. Pressed together on the couch were his mother, Venus, his 16-year-old sister, Tamara, Grandma, and Aunt Amelia. His 20-year-old sister, Yolanda, sat in a chair holding her infant son. Peter's five-year-old brother, Sam, was playing Candyland with his four cousins, ages two through seven, in the corner of the room.

Suddenly, the front door opened, and a burst of wind-swept rain blew into the house. Peter's 23-year-old brother, Jerome, scurried inside. His shirt, jeans, and baseball cap were sopping wet. "You need to leave here for a shelter right now," he announced. "The storm is turning into a monster."

"Maybe you're right," Peter's mother said. "I think we should get out of here and go to higher ground farther inland, out in the country."

"Momma, we'll be fine here," said Peter. "We rode out Ivan, and we didn't have any problems. Why should this be any different?"

"I agree with Peter," Grandma said. "This house of mine has stood here for over thirty years and gone through many storms before. The cement blocks under here will keep us high and dry."

"But, Grandma, they say this could be the baddest one of all," Jerome warned. "All of you, come with me, please. There's a shelter at the homeless mission about six blocks from here. You'll be safer there because it's on higher ground. I can make a couple of trips in my car so that everyone can get to the shelter. "

"I don't want to be stuck in a crowded shelter with strangers," Peter argued. The adults, except for his mother, nodded in agreement.

"Y'all are free to go," Grandma said to the others, "but we're better off here than out in that wind and rain."

Jerome pleaded with the adults, but finally gave up in frustration. Even his mother decided to stay. Bending down, Jerome looked directly into Peter's eyes and whispered, "Look around you, Peter. You see small children, old ladies, and women who panic easily, except for maybe Tamara. Do you really think they can take care of themselves in an emergency? When this place blows down or gets flooded — and one or the other will happen — guess who's going to have to take charge? I'm telling you, before this storm is over, you'll be in a tighter spot than any of those superheroes you read about in your comic books."

"We're staying," Peter insisted. "We'll be fine."

Peter couldn't have been more wrong. Jerome couldn't have been more right.

Shortly after Jerome left, the power went out, causing Prissy to let out a shriek, which frightened the younger ones.

"We might as well turn in for the night," said Grandma. "Not much else we can do in the dark." She pulled out a flashlight and helped get everyone situated.

The house had only one bedroom, so Amelia, Yolanda, Tamara, and the children slept on chairs, rugs, and the couch in the living room. With his dog, Duke, Peter sprawled out on a blanket on the floor at the foot of a bed that was shared by his mother, Grandmother, and Prissy. *Nothing to worry about,* Peter thought before falling into a deep slumber.

Shortly before dawn, his mother shook Peter. "Peter, wake up! Water is coming into the house!"

Once the grogginess cleared his head, he realized that the blanket he was sleeping on was soaked. His mother shined a flashlight on the floor, revealing about an inch of water. Duke was pacing and panting nervously.

"Peter, I was afraid you were going to drown in your sleep," his mother said. He could hardly hear her over the deafening roar of the wind. From the loud banging overhead, he knew that fierce gusts were peeling back part of the tin roof.

Katrina sounds a lot worse than Ivan, he thought. *A lot worse.*

Peter took the flashlight and aimed it out the window. *Uh-oh, it definitely is worse.* Floodwater had nearly swallowed up the family car; only its roof was visible. Feeling a strange sensation in his bare feet, he looked down and saw water seeping up between the floorboards. *This is getting bad.* For the first time since the storm struck, Peter was worried.

Meanwhile, Yolanda and Tamara were waking up the children, hustling them into the kitchen, and putting them on the counter to stay dry.

Back in the bedroom, Peter's mother shouted to Grandma, who was stirring awake. "Momma, the roof is tearing off the house, and water is coming up through the floor! We've got to get out of here!"

"Oh, girl, lie down and go back to sleep," Grandma, still half asleep, mumbled.

Peter shook her and said, "Grandma, Momma is right. You have to get up. It's not safe here anymore."

His mother turned to Peter and wailed, "What are we going to do?"

The deafening noise from the screaming wind, rattling roof, and whimpering children made it hard for him to concentrate. *Stop, stop!* he thought. *I wish it would all stop!* He cupped his hands over his ears. *Think of something. They're all counting on me.*

Meanwhile, Tamara grabbed the phone and exclaimed, "It's still working!"

"Call nine-one-one," Peter said.

She did and then blurted into the phone, "Help us! There are nine children and four adults here at two zero zero three

Dogwood Avenue, and we're trapped. Water is coming up so fast we can't get out. Send help! Hurry!"

Her look of distress turned to alarm as she hung up the phone. "They said there isn't anyone who can help us. It's too dangerous. They said we're on our own. Now what will we do?"

"There isn't anything we can do except stay where we are," Grandma replied.

The house was rocking and creaking from the howling and ever-strengthening wind and rising storm surge. Water from the damaged roof was dripping steadily from various spots in the ceiling.

Peter shined the flashlight out the window. The street had turned into a raging white-capped river. Looking about 100 feet past the submerged car, he saw that the house of the next-door neighbors, the Wilsons, was on higher ground. Although only one story tall, the house was made of cement block, so Peter figured it would likely withstand Katrina's wrath. His grandmother's house was an older, wooden A-frame.

"Momma, we need to get to the Wilsons'," Peter said.

"But that means we have to swim in that flood." She shook her head. "We'll all drown."

"We have no choice," he declared. "We can't stay here. The flood is getting higher. I don't know how long we have before the house gets knocked off its foundation."

After ushering everyone into the kitchen, Peter asked, "Who knows how to swim?" He raised his hand. No one else did, although Tamara raised hers halfway and said, "I *sorta* know how to float."

Hearing the question, Prissy murmured "Oh, no, oh, no." She began to cry, triggering tears in the smaller children.

"We'll just hold on to each other real tight and wade in the water over to the Wilson's," said Peter. "At least the current of the flood is heading in the right direction."

The adults protested. "Let's wait a little while longer," Grandma suggested. "The storm should be easing up soon."

It didn't. As daylight came, Katrina intensified, and the storm surge kept rising until it was about six inches above the windowsills. Water was seeping through the cracks and out-lets in the wall. Worse yet, the house began to tilt.

"We can't wait any longer," said Peter. "The house will be swept away any moment. We need to get everybody out now!"

The water in the house was above the knees of the adults. Chairs and tables were beginning to float around the living room. Duke could barely keep his head above the surface.

"Our babies! Our babies!" Peter's mother wailed. "What's going to happen to them?"

It was time for Peter to take charge of their escape.

"Yolanda, make sure the little ones stay put on the kitchen counter," he said. "Tamara, gather up all the sheets. We'll rip them into strips and make a rope out of them. Then we'll walk out of here all tied together so no one will slip away."

After they prepared the sheet-rope, they wrapped it around one another. But the pressure from the storm surge made it impossible to open the front door. "How will we get out of here?" asked Aunt Amelia.

After they untied themselves, Peter ordered everyone into

the kitchen and off the floor. Then he picked up a chair and smashed the double-wide window in the living room. Brackish, smelly water gushed in, knocking Peter down, upending furniture, and shoving Duke into the kitchen where the others were bawling. When the water level inside the house was even with the storm surge outside, Peter broke off the jagged edges of the window so it would be safer to exit.

They tied themselves together again. Yolanda, the tallest of the group, held her baby and stepped out into the surging water. "The current is too strong!" she yelled. "Pull me back!" The others yanked her into the house.

"We're going to die!" Prissy sobbed. "I know it. We're all going to die!"

"Not if I can help it," Peter retorted. "Now shut up!"

"Peter," said Tamara. "Do you think we can each take one kid at a time and swim over to the Wilsons' house?"

"Better let me do it," he replied. "No offense, but you swim like a rock."

Before moving the children, Peter decided to take Yolanda over first so she could watch after them when he brought them to the Wilsons'. He tied the sheet-rope around Yolanda and himself and told her, "Hold my hand. We're going to let the current push us to the Wilsons'."

"I'll try to be brave," she stammered.

They crawled out the window and were swiftly carried by the storm surge toward the Wilsons'. Paddling by Peter's side was Duke, who had slipped out the open window so he could remain by his master.

When they reached the Wilsons' front porch, Peter grabbed

the railing and pulled himself and his sister onto the stoop. The Wilsons weren't home, so Peter and Yolanda kicked in the front door.

Then Peter swam back toward his grandmother's house. But fighting the swift current wasn't easy. Tall and lanky for his age, the boy was glad that he had been working out with weights at his middle school, because he needed all the arm strength he had built up. Duke huffed but managed to keep pace with him during his return.

Inside Grandma's house, Peter cradled the youngest child in one arm and went out the window. Using a sidestroke, he swam to the Wilsons' and handed the child to Yolanda. One by one, he ferried the youngsters to his older sister while his faithful dog escorted him.

Several times he had to dodge floating debris — tree limbs, furniture, a refrigerator, and rubble from smashed houses. It finally became too hazardous for the dog to swim with him, so Peter ordered Duke to stay on the Wilsons' porch. The dog whined and barked in protest but obeyed his master.

Meanwhile, Tamara was trying to keep her mother, grandmother, and younger sister calm. Prissy was squatting on the stove, weeping. Crouched on top of the kitchen counter, Grandma clutched Peter's mother and said, "I guess this is the way we're going to die. We'll drown."

"I don't want to die like this, Momma," she wailed.

"You can't give up," Tamara said. "Everything is going to be all right. You'll see."

Peter waded into the kitchen and said, "Grandma, you're next."

"No, I can't do it," she objected. "I'll drown for sure. I'm too big and too scared. Save Prissy. Save your momma. Just leave me behind."

"You and Tamara take Prissy," their mother ordered. "Grandma and I will leave our lives in God's hands. Now go, Peter!"

"No way," he said. "Not without all of you."

The rushing water, which was now up to his neck, had ripped the front door off its hinges. He grabbed it and positioned it next to the kitchen counter. "Get on it, Grandma," he said.

"Oh, I'm afraid . . ."

"Just do it!" he commanded, surprising himself with the forcefulness of his voice. Shaking from fear, the 200-pound woman leaned over and belly flopped on the door, grasping it for dear life. Then holding it from the back end like a boogie board, Peter began kicking and maneuvered the door out the window and into the floodwater.

Grandma never stopped screaming until Peter brought her safely to the Wilsons'. But when he tried to swim back with the door, the fierce current ripped it out of his hands.

Stroking harder and harder, he couldn't understand why he wasn't making any progress. Something was holding him back. The rushing water slapped him in the face and then surged over his head. He struggled to get his nose above the surface as wave after wave slammed into him.

Prissy, who was clutching the side of the broken window, screamed, "Oh, no! Peter is going under! I can't see him! He's drowning!"

He finally realized that his shirt had become snagged on

a submerged tree limb. "Don't ... *glub* ... worry, Prissy ... *glub* ... I'm coming to get you!"

Taking a deep breath, he went underwater, took off his shirt, and freed himself from the limb. Then he swam to his shivering, panic-stricken sister.

"Let go of the windowsill and come into my arms," he told her.

"No ... I can't ... I'll drown!"

"Just wrap your arms around my neck. You have to let go. I'm getting tired of treading water."

"No, let me stay here!"

He climbed onto the windowsill. "Prissy, come with me."

She shook her head, her eyes wide with fright. Out of patience, Peter pried her fingers off the windowsill one at a time and pulled her into the water. His petrified sister screamed and squeezed her arms around his neck so hard he could barely breathe all the way to the Wilsons'.

Then he returned for his mother, who was gripping Tamara's hand as they stood on the kitchen table. "I don't think I can do this," his mother said. By now the water inside was over Peter's head and the house had tilted at a severe angle. "Momma, get down here and I'll guide you out, just like I have for all the others. This house is about to come apart."

"Oh, I don't know. . . ."

In his frustration, he leaped up, grabbed her by the hand, and yanked her into the water.

"What are you doing?" she gasped.

"Trying to save your life. You're coming with me."

27

Tamara jumped into the water, too. The three of them tied the sheet-rope around one another and floated toward the open window. Although his mother weighed three times as much as Peter, she clasped her arms around his back, and they, along with Tamara, floated to the Wilsons'.

When everyone was safe in the house, Grandma shouted, "You did it, Peter! You're our hero!"

"Oh, Mama, look!" wailed his mother. Everyone crowded around the window. The power of the storm surge had finally pushed Grandma's house off its foundation and shoved it into the side of the Wilsons' house. It took only minutes before her beloved home broke apart in a series of heartbreaking cracks and snaps. And just like that, all her worldly possessions spilled into the rushing water and were carried away forever.

"Oh, your house!" Peter's mother cried. "It's gone! You've lost everything!"

"No, not everything," said Grandma. "Just *things.* I still have all of you." Then her lip quivered and she broke down and sobbed.

The wind, although strong, had lessened considerably. The storm surge, however, was still rising and had reached the front door of the Wilsons'. *We might have to leave here, but where will we go?* Peter wondered. Then he spotted a small flat-bottom boat drifting aimlessly in the flood about 100 yards away. He jumped in the water — and so did Duke, who could no longer bear the thought of watching his young master swim alone. Peter reached the boat, climbed inside, and pulled his dog in with him. He started paddling with his hands but didn't get anywhere. Spotting a broom on the porch of a nearby house, he jumped out, snatched it, then got back into the boat and used the broom as his paddle.

Trying to find help, Peter headed to a major intersection, which was now under at least 15 feet of water, but he saw no one. He returned to the Wilsons', where the rising water was now seeping in. "We need to leave this place," he announced.

"Where will we go now?" Grandma asked.

"The old apartment building," he replied. Peter was referring to an abandoned three-story structure that was a few doors down from the Wilsons'. Over the next half hour, he shuttled his relatives in the boat to the building where they huddled together on the top floor to wait out the storm. By mid-morning, the floodwaters had crested and the winds had weakened.

Peter and his family survived Hurricane Katrina — the most destructive storm in American history. It claimed more than sixteen hundred lives (with more than one thousand people unaccounted for) and caused an estimated seventy-five billion dollars in damage. The hurricane also left more than 1.5 million people homeless — a humanitarian crisis unseen before in the United States.

Katrina's ferocious winds and 30-foot-high storm surge killed about 100 people in the Biloxi area and destroyed or seriously damaged more than 60 percent of the city's homes and businesses. Historic mansions and magnificent multimillion-dollar casinos were trashed beyond recognition.

Like thousands of other citizens in Biloxi, Peter and his family were left without anything but their lives. Their homes were destroyed or washed away along with virtually all their belongings. As survivors, they were forced to move into shelters and temporary housing. But they were still thankful that they had one another.

When they reunited with Jerome at a Biloxi shelter, Peter's mother put her arms around her sons and told Jerome, "I just thank God for Peter. We would not be here but for the grace of God and Peter's courage. He's our hero."

Jerome rubbed his brother's head and said, "Better than any comic-book superhero, huh, Peter?"

THE EDGE OF
DISASTER

"**A**re you going to finish those fries?" Mack Worthy asked his friend Darrel Spires.

Darrel shook his head and shoved the half-full pouch of McDonald's fries across the length of the table. "You can have them."

"Thanks," said Mack, who sat in a chair at the end of the table because he was too large to fit comfortably in the restaurant booth. Looking at their buddy Ray Huggins, he asked, "What about the rest of your burger?"

"You want my half-eaten burger?" responded Ray with a bewildered look.

"As long as you don't have any germs."

"I'm disease-free," Ray assured him. Then, shaking his head, Ray repeated, "You want my half-eaten burger?"

"You're not eating it, and I'd hate for it to go to waste," said Mack.

31

"Nothing goes to waste when you're around," cracked the fourth member of the group, Johnny Huggins, Ray's cousin.

"I'm a growing boy — and I'm growing a lot more than you two runts," he retorted, pointing to the cousins. "Heck, Ray, you're so skinny you could hula hoop inside a Fruit Loop."

The boys, all sixth graders at Amory Middle School in Mississippi, often traded good-natured barbs at one another. On this particular Saturday, they were eating lunch at McDonald's, spending some of the money they had earned earlier that morning. They had cleaned out junk from a ratty apartment building that the fathers of Ray and Johnny had recently bought to fix up.

The two cousins were best friends and often spent time with Darrel. Although Darrel was in the same class, he was a year older than the others because he had to repeat second grade. Occasionally, they would invite Mack to come along with them. However, because Mack was so overweight, he seldom could keep up with them, especially when they were whizzing around town on their bikes or playing hoops on the school playground. But Mack was a kindhearted, likable kid, and fun to be around.

Besides, whenever they had paintball wars on the Huggins family property, the boys wanted Mack on their team because he possessed a shooter's eye. The downside: He was a large, slow-moving target for the enemy.

"Hey, Mack, I've got one fry left," Johnny said. "You want it?"

Mack started to reach for it and then held up. "Nah, I'm cutting back on my calories," he replied with a wink. Mack often made fun of himself to take the sting out of jokes about his weight or his love of eating.

Darrel, who had a bad habit of pushing things too far, shoved over an empty hamburger wrapper. "Want this? It doesn't have any calories."

"Go fly a kite, Darrel," Mack snapped.

Trying to defuse a potential conflict, Ray piped up, "Hey, that's a great idea. Let's all go fly kites up on the bluffs."

"Better yet, let's have a kite-fighting contest and try to knock each other's kites out of the sky," Johnny suggested. The others thought it was a great idea.

"With the money we made today, we can buy a bunch of cheap kites at Topper's down the street," Ray said.

"How will we get to the bluffs?" asked Mack.

Johnny replied, "We can take our bi . . ." He looked at Mack and stopped in mid-sentence. *There's no way Mack could bike two miles up the hill to the bluffs. But we can't go without him. It wouldn't be right.* "I think I can get my brother to take us up there in his pickup. He owes me a favor. I didn't squeal on him for sneaking into the house way past curfew last weekend."

The boys bought two kites each and within the hour were at the bluffs — a flat area thick with pine trees except for a ten-acre clearing that ended in a 100-foot drop to an icy stream. Johnny's brother, Mike, reluctantly had taken the boys there (Darrel and Mack had to sit outside in the back of the truck) and told them he would return at 4 P.M. to pick them up. A brisk north wind made the bright January day seem ten degrees cooler than the actual temperature, but it was perfect for kite-fighting.

"The rules are simple," Johnny explained. "You have to force down the other guy's kite. You can do this by crashing your kite into his kite so it tips over and falls to the ground. Or you can use your kite's line to cut your opponent's line and make it crash. If your kite gets banged up, you can fix it and stay in the fight as long as your kite doesn't touch the ground."

"You might as well declare me the winner now," Darrel boasted. "Nobody can beat me."

Running into the breeze, the four boys pulled on their strings, and soon the kites were rocketing into the sky. Holding on to their spools, the competitors dashed left and right (except for Mack, who sort of waddled), working hard to get an advantage. The kites glided and spun and made broad sweeps across the winter sky.

During the first round, which lasted nearly twenty minutes, the competitors darted around the clearing and one another, making sure to stay away from the edge of the cliff.

Ray tried to maneuver his kite so that his line would wrap around the string on Johnny's kite that was securing the center and cross spars. Meanwhile, Darrel moved his kite into a position so it tipped Mack's kite and forced it to the ground. Mack was much too slow to save his kite before it smashed.

"You're out, Mack!" Darrel shouted gleefully.

"I'll get even," grumbled Mack. "Just you wait."

Darrel then skillfully directed his kite against Ray's line, hoping to generate heat by having the two lines rub against each other. Ray's line eventually frayed enough so that it broke, making his kite uncontrollable.

"I got you!" Darrel declared.

"Not so fast. As long as my kite doesn't touch the ground, I'm still alive."

Unable to control it, Ray tried to yank his kite so it would slam into Darrel's. When that failed, he tried to tangle up Darrel's main line and drag it to the ground. But Darrel was too nimble and fast and ran out of the way while remaining aware of how close he was to the edge of the cliff. Seconds later, Ray's kite nose-dived into the ground about ten feet from the sheer drop.

"Hey, Johnny, it's just you and me now," Darrel said. The two boys tried to show off their skills by lowering their kites close to the ground so that the fight would end quicker. Darrel rammed his kite into Johnny's kite, causing Johnny's to go into a tailspin. Johnny ran after it and caught the kite just a few inches above the ground. "I'm not out of it yet!" he shouted. He retied a broken string and launched his kite again. But it didn't fly for long. Darrel managed to cut Johnny's string, sending the kite out of reach as it flew beyond the lip of the bluff and eventually fluttered into the stream far below.

"The winner!" Darrel shouted. "I'm the king of the kites!"

"Not for long," said Johnny, rigging up his spare kite.

Still flying his slightly battered kite, Darrel found himself the number one target as the three other boys attacked him. Jerking and tugging on their lines, the boys squinted into the bright winter sky as they jockeyed for position. Slamming their kites into Darrel's, they succeeded in driving it into the frozen dirt. Then Johnny and Ray battled each other. But their lines tangled into such a mess that both their kites plunged to the ground before they could save them. Mack won that match by simply staying out of the way of the others.

In the third round, the other boys ganged up on Mack. Like sharks circling their prey, the kites closed in on Mack's and struck it repeatedly and finally sent it spiraling out of control and over the cliff. The kite fight continued for another ten minutes until Johnny came away the winner.

The next match went to Ray, who used a nifty move to wrap his line around Darrel's kite and drag it to the ground.

"We've each won a round," Darrel said. "Whoever wins the next one is declared the king of the kites — unless, of course, you want to name me the winner now and save yourselves further embarrassment."

"You're going to end up as red as your kite," taunted Ray.

The boys each licked a finger and held it up to test the direction of the shifting wind. They launched their kites and wasted no time attacking one another.

Mack tried to remain above the fighting, assuming the others would knock one another out, but they figured out his strategy and ganged up on him. His kite was the first to bust apart. Mack wasn't all that upset because he was tired, anyway, so he plopped down on a large rock to watch the rest of the contest.

"Oh, no, not again!" moaned Johnny. The main string broke, and all he could do was watch his kite waffle in the breeze before it disappeared over the side of the cliff.

Now it was Darrel against Ray. "You're going to lose. You know you are," Darrel chided him.

"Not on your life!"

Their two kites dipped and dived and swirled around in big loops. The boys' legs ached, their necks stiffened, and their fingers froze, yet neither would give in. Darrel was competitive in whatever he did — whether it was a game of Horse or Uno. He *had* to win. Ray was also competitive, but because of his slight build and a lack of coordination, he seldom won any physical contests. Although he had a lot of heart, he usually came up short. And more often than not, he lost to Darrel.

Not this time, Ray told himself. *I'm not going to let him beat me. Concentrate, be patient, and play it smart.* He didn't dare take his eyes off the two kites. *Release some line. Now pull it in. Run. I'm going to get him!*

"Hey, Ray, you're getting close to the edge of the cliff," warned Darrel.

Don't listen to him, Ray thought. *He's just trying to distract you. Stay focused.*

"Ray, be careful!" Mack shouted. "Look where you're going!"

Gee, Mack is on Darrel's side, too? Stay focused.

A gust of wind lifted Ray's kite over Darrel's, and Ray was in excellent position to attack it. When Ray heard Darrel mutter, "Oh, oh," Ray sensed the end was at hand. *I'll finally beat him at something.* Ray backpedaled a little bit more and jerked on the string. *Yes!*

"Ray, look out!" Mack and Johnny shouted in alarm.

I've got him! Ray's kite slammed into Darrel's at a right angle, cutting a vital string on the cross spar, and causing it to spin wildly out of control.

"Ray! No!"

Yes! Yes! He's going down!

Ray took one more backward step and suddenly found himself slipping off the lip of the bluff. The top face of the cliff angled out at a 45-degree slant for the first ten feet before it turned into a straight vertical drop.

Ray let go of his spool and began sliding down chest-first on the angled part of the bluff. Clawing at rocks and clumps of brush in a desperate attempt to slow down his descent, Ray let out a bloodcurdling scream, "Aaaahhhh!"

I'm going to die!

At the last possible moment before he was about to plunge nearly 100 feet to an almost certain death, Ray grasped hold of the stump of a small tree no more than four inches in diameter. It was about a foot from where the slanting top of the cliff face turned into a deadly vertical drop.

With his feet dangling over the side, Ray let out a lengthy, terrified cry. "Help!" *This can't really be happening to me. Please, oh please, God, don't let this stump pull out.*

The boys rushed over to the edge and peered down. Seeing their frightened buddy hanging onto the stump, Mack felt like throwing up.

"We'll save you, Ray!" Darrel shouted down. "Hang on!"

"What can we do?" Johnny whispered to his pals. "My brother won't be back for another half hour."

"Ray can't hold on that long," Darrel said. "We can't leave him there and run for help." After a quick survey of the situation, he added, "Let me try."

Darrel lay on his stomach, reached over the edge, and grasped the trunk of a small bush two feet below the top of the bluff. Then he lowered himself down the angled slope until he hung by his hands on the trunk.

I can't believe I'm doing this, Darrel thought. "Ray, can you reach my feet?"

"I'm afraid to let go with one hand," said Ray. "Can't you get any closer?"

Any closer and I might fall off the cliff, Darrel thought. He spotted a little ledge below him and off to the right. It jutted out from the cliff face by only a few inches. Darrel grabbed another small tree that was growing above the ledge and carefully lowered himself so he could stand on the ledge and be closer to Ray. Removing his left hand from the tree, Darrel leaned down and said, "Ray, give me your right hand."

"I'm too scared to let go," said Ray, his face pressed against the side of the bluff.

"You can do it. Come on. My hand is only a foot away from the stump you're holding on to."

Ray glanced up and then took a peek below.

"Don't look down!" Darrel ordered. "Look at me! On the count of three, grab my hand! One . . . two . . . three!"

Ray took a deep breath and pulled on the stump, trying to get a little lift while releasing his right hand. He felt Darrel's left hand clasp around his right wrist. Just then the stump that Ray was holding started coming lose, sending frozen balls of dirt onto Ray's head.

"I've got you!" Darrel said.

After Ray gripped his other hand onto Darrel's left wrist, Ray's legs swayed in the air. With a mighty tug from Darrel, Ray managed to get a little toehold on a tiny outcropping, easing the strain on Darrel's arms.

"Keep cool, okay?" said Darrel, who was holding on to the tree with his right hand and Ray with his left.

"I'm trying, but it's not easy. How about you?"

"I'm okay, although both my arms feel like they're going to come out of their sockets soon."

"Now what do we do?" Ray asked.

Darrel shouted up to Mack and Johnny, "Any ideas?"

"Can you climb back up?" Johnny asked.

"No, not while I'm holding Ray."

"There's got to be a way," Mack told Johnny. "What if we wrap all the kite string from our spools together and make a rope?"

"It won't be strong enough to hold those two."

After a few seconds of thought, Mack asked, "Johnny, does being upside down bother you?"

"Why are you asking me that at a time like this?"

"I have a plan," Mack declared. "We're going to make a human chain."

"Are you crazy?"

"Probably. But we have no other choice, Johnny. I'll be the anchor."

"And that makes me . . . ?"

"The most important link in the human chain."

"But, Mack, what if you lose your grip on me?"

"Then you'll probably die. And so will Ray and Darrel. But I'm not going to let that happen."

A tree stump about six inches in diameter poked out of the ground a few feet from the edge of the cliff. Mack lay on his belly between the stump and the edge. He wrapped his legs around the stump and locked his feet while stretching his arms toward the cliff face. Johnny then lay on his stomach in front of Mack. Johnny's chest and arms were well over the edge while Mack held on to Johnny's ankles.

"Are you sure you can hold on to me?" Johnny asked.

"I outweigh you by about fifty pounds. I'm sure."

Johnny then slid headfirst down the slope until his hands could reach the tree that Darrel was holding. With a firm grip on Johnny's ankles, Mack dug his elbows into the cold ground at the top of the bluff. Both boys had the exact same thought: *Don't let go.*

"Ray, you need to climb up to Darrel so you can reach my hand," said Johnny. "Hurry because the blood is rushing to my head and it's making me dizzy."

"I'll help you," Darrel told Ray before pulling him up beside him on the ledge. "Okay, Ray. Let go of my hand and grab Johnny's hands."

"I'm afraid to let go."

"Come on, Ray. It's the only way."

Ray hesitantly extended his left hand to Johnny, who took hold of it. Removing his other hand from Darrel's wrist, Ray gripped Johnny's other hand.

"Okay, Mack!" shouted Johnny. "Lift us up!"

Mack had no trouble holding on to Johnny. But with the added weight from Ray, Mack found it a lot more difficult. *I've got to hold on,* Mack told himself. *Pull, Mack! Pull!* His arms and legs shaking from the exertion, Mack slowly wriggled backward, rose to a kneeling position, and hauled Johnny and Ray upward a few inches at a time. Like the anchor in a contest of a tug-of-war, Mack huffed and grunted and kept yanking until both Johnny and Ray were safely over the top.

Ray sprawled out on the ground and wept. "I'm safe! Hallelujah, I'm safe!"

Mack, who was on his knees, bowed his head in relief. He turned to Johnny and asked, "You doing okay?"

Using the back of his hand to blot his bloody chin, Johnny said, "I banged my head on a rock when you were pulling me up. I'm pretty dizzy, too, but otherwise I'm fine."

"Hey, up there!" shouted Darrel. "Quit yakking and get me out of here!"

The boys scrambled to the edge. Once again, Johnny slid over the top of the cliff on his stomach and reached out for Darrel while Mack held on to Johnny's ankles. Seconds later, Mack, with help from Ray, pulled Darrel and Johnny up and over the bluff.

"We did it!" shouted Johnny. "We did it!"

Ray hugged Mack, Johnny, and Darrel. "Thank you, guys, for risking your lives. I thought for sure I was a goner."

"I didn't really risk mine," Mack said.

"Maybe so," said Darrel, "but if it hadn't been for you, we wouldn't have been able to get off the cliff face."

"It's a good thing you're as big as you are, Mack," Johnny said. "No one else could have anchored the human chain."

"Well, it's also a good thing you and Ray are runts," Mack said.

Ray, who was still shaking from his close encounter with death, told his buddies, "I don't know how I'll ever repay you guys."

"For me, that's easy," Darrel said. "Admit that I'm the king of kites."

"But I beat you. I knocked your kite out of the sky."

"Your kite went down, too."

Ray's shoulders slumped. *He's right. I didn't win after all.*

"Hey, look over there," said Johnny, pointing to a tree about 20 yards from the edge of the cliff. The main string of Ray's kite had snagged on an upper branch. The steady breeze had kept the kite dancing in the air out over the bluff.

"Look at that!" shouted Ray. "My kite never hit the ground." He raised his arms in triumph. "That makes me the king of kites!"

Rubbing his ample belly, Mack said, "I'll eat to that!"

ON THIN ICE

Fastened to a tall wooden post in the frozen pond was a sign. The message couldn't have been clearer. The letters were painted big and bold in red on a white background. DANGER! STAY OFF THE ICE!

But the neighborhood kids tended to ignore the warning. This was February in Massachusetts, the best time to skate and play hockey on a frozen pond. Players liked to joke that if you fell through the ice, save the puck first because it's much easier to find a submerged kid than a sinking puck.

Most everyone who skated or walked on this particular ice-covered pond knew ice should be at least four inches thick to be safe, although the thickness and strength varied. One area of the pond could have ice a foot thick while another part could be only an inch solid. The kids knew that new ice was usually stronger than old ice; that rain and wind can thin or weaken ice. Every once in a while, someone would test the ice too early in the winter and drop through. "Doing the dunk" — as the kids called it — typically happened in shallow water, so the consequence was nothing more serious than a teeth-chattering ice bath and a lot of teasing.

But that wasn't true for Laurie Robertson and her little brother, Calvin. Had it not been for Little Miss Know-It-All, they would have died a slow, horrible death.

Little Miss Know-It-All was the nickname that students at Hamilton Elementary placed on Bebe Jacobs, a bright but socially awkward fourth grader. A loner by nature, the gawky brunette had few friends, partly because she appeared to her fellow students as bossy, impatient, and snobbish. When a kid in class would answer a question incorrectly or ask what Bebe considered a dumb question, she would shake her head. She further annoyed classmates by raising her hand at every question the teacher asked. No one could remember the last time she was ever wrong. That's why they called her Little Miss Know-It-All.

Bebe wasn't trying to show off her knowledge so much as test it. She had a hungry mind that needed constant stimulation. Her favorite room in school was the library. Always looking to expand her mind, she read magazines about astronomy, biology, and archaeology. She pored over articles in *The New York Times* and *Boston Globe*. On her own, she began teaching herself French. She never went anywhere without a book under her arm. She read on the bus, in the cafeteria, and on the playground. During recess, when the other kids were playing kickball or hanging from the monkey bars, Bebe would sit under a tree and read a book, something challenging such as Shakespeare. (She had already read many of the classics such as *Moby Dick, Treasure Island,* and *Little Women* by the second grade.)

As the school's top bookworm, Bebe was an easy target for lame practical jokes. One morning, two boys caught a beetle in the room before class and put it in her desk. When she opened the desk top and saw the insect, she screamed, igniting a round of uproarious laughter. Another time, a student bumped into her and, while apologizing to her, nimbly taped a paper sign on her back that read, LAUGH AT ME. Bebe couldn't understand why kids were giggling and pointing at her throughout recess, until a teacher went over and took the sign off her.

Although the pranks hurt Bebe's feelings, she wouldn't cry or retaliate. She would adjust her glasses, squeeze her lips, and pretend it never happened. She would walk away with her head held high in what she thought was a show of poise and self-confidence. But to many students at Hamilton, her attitude made them think she was snooty and stuck-up.

So it came as no surprise when someone sneaked into her desk while everyone was in art class — the final period of the day — and stole her notebook. Bebe had remained after the art class for ten minutes to complete her lovely still-life watercolor. When she returned to her empty homeroom to gather her books, she found a note in her desk saying, "If you want your notebook, go to the last stall in the boys' bathroom."

Morons, Bebe thought. *These jerks just can't stand the fact that I'm smart and they're dumb. Should I go to the teacher with this? What for? Mrs. Long never found out who put the beetle in my desk. If I make a stink, the other kids will just hate me more than they already do now. I need to take care of this on my own.*

While students were leaving the building, Bebe camped out by the boys' bathroom and waited until she was sure no one was inside. *Well, it's now or never.* She whipped open the door, scurried inside, and went to the last stall. Instead of her notebook, she found a sign taped to the wall that said BEBE WAS HERE.

In smaller letters was another note: "Your notebook is somewhere in the bathroom." She opened the doors to the other stalls and searched under the sinks without any luck. Only after she took the top off the tall trash container and sifted around in the wadded up paper towels did she find her notebook. While she was retrieving it, the door to the bathroom opened. Afraid to be seen, Bebe tried to hide behind the trash container, but it was too small to conceal her.

"What in the world are you doing in here?" bellowed Mr. Wright, the principal.

"I was getting my notebook, sir."

"Young lady, come with me."

By the time Bebe explained what had happened, she had missed her bus, so she headed home on foot. She figured the walk would do her good. It gave her a chance to collect her thoughts over why she was being picked on and what she was going to do about it. *I wish I could fit in,* she told herself. *I wish someone could understand what it feels like to be me. I can't help it that I'm so smart.*

The house she shared with her divorced mother was about a mile away by taking the shortcut through the forest preserve. For a winter day, it was fairly pleasant — partly cloudy, temperatures in the high thirties. Some of the snow from a winter storm earlier in the week had melted and the remaining snow was slushy. Bebe zipped her down jacket up to her neck and was glad she had decided to wear her calf-length boots that day. They would keep her feet dry when she hiked through the preserve.

It was a safe, popular area bordered on the north and east by houses. When she neared the frozen pond, she was surprised no one was playing hockey or skating. *Of course*, she thought. *The ice is too thin from all the melting we've had the last few days.*

However, two children who she recognized were playing on the ice near the edge of the bank. Neighborhood kids Laurie Robertson, eight, and her brother, Calvin, six, were throwing snowballs at each other.

"Hey, you two better get off there!" Bebe shouted. "If you don't, you're going to fall through the ice."

"We don't have to listen to you, Little Miss Know-It-All," Laurie sassed back.

Pointing to the warning sign jutting out of the frozen pond, Bebe said, "You're old enough to read."

"Leave us alone!" Calvin snapped.

"Suit yourself, but you're walking on very thin ice," Bebe retorted. She frowned, shook her head and walked on. Seconds later . . . *SPLAT!* A snowball slammed into her back. She turned around and . . . *SPLAT!* . . . another one hit her square in the face, knocking off her glasses. "Stop it!" she commanded. Bebe groped in the mushy snow for her glasses, picked them up, and started to clean them off, when she got hit again. "That does it! Now I'm mad!"

Dropping her books, Bebe ran to the edge of the pond. Calvin moved warily out to the middle. Laurie, who held snowballs in each hand, had retreated, too, and was now between him and Bebe.

Not wanting to step out onto the ice, Bebe held her hands out and said, "What's wrong with you idiots?"

"Oh, is Little Miss Know-It-All going to cry?" said Laurie in a nasty singsong tone.

"Of course not. Why would you throw snowballs at me? I've never done anything to either one of you."

"We were just having a little harmless fun."

"It's not so harmless. And quite frankly I'm getting sick and tired of it." Bebe backed away from the pond, keeping her eyes on both kids. They made no attempt to fling another snowball at her, although they made mean faces. Bebe picked up her books, brushed the snow off of them, and continued on the path toward her house.

As Bebe walked away, Calvin jumped up and down on the frozen pond. He put a thumb in each ear, waved his fingers, and stuck his tongue out at Bebe. "Nah-nee, nah-nee, boo-boo," he taunted.

Bebe turned around and told Laurie, "You better go get your brother before he falls through the ice."

"Whatever you say, Little Miss Know-It-All."

"Nah-nee, nah-nee, boo-boo," Calvin teased one more time.

As Bebe entered a thick stand of pines about 100 yards

from the pond, she heard a scream. "Calvin! Oh, my God, Calvin!" Bebe stopped and cocked her ear to listen. There was silence for several seconds. And then she heard Laurie yell, "Help! Somebody, help!"

Bebe spun around and ran back to the pond. She saw Laurie in the middle of the pond, waving her arms and shouting. A few feet away from the girl was a hole in the ice where Calvin was flopping around in the water.

Flinging her books aside, Bebe started to walk gingerly on the pond when she heard a loud crack and saw Laurie plunge through the ice and into the water.

"Oh, no!" shouted Bebe. Scanning in all four directions for someone but seeing no one, she yelled anyway. "Help! Help!"

There's no one else around, she told herself. *I've got to save them myself. A branch. I need a branch.* She scurried around, trying to find one long and sturdy enough to work. "Keep your head above water!" she shouted to them.

The depth of the pond was about 15 feet in the center. Fortunately, Calvin and Laurie knew how to swim. But with their bulky winter gear soaked and filling with icy water, they could barely keep from going under.

As the cold shock response set in, they began gasping and hyperventilating. Their bodies were reacting to the plunge into deadly cold water, which draws out heat from a person at a rate 25 times faster than cold air.

Both children were clawing at the edges of the holes they had created when they fell in. But each time they held on to the ice, it broke off. Their breathing was so labored they couldn't talk or shout or do anything but grunt.

"Don't give up!" Bebe shouted. "I'll get you out!"

After seizing a broken limb from a maple tree, Bebe carefully shuffled her way toward the middle of the frozen pond. She held her breath every time the ice below her groaned and cracked. *I hope the ice doesn't break underneath me. What should I do so that won't happen? Oh, yes, get down on my stomach and spread out the weight.* She crawled on her belly until she was about four feet from Laurie and held out the branch. "Grab it and I'll pull you out!" Bebe shouted. Laurie held on to the branch, and Bebe started to pull. But the ice was wet and slippery and she had no traction. Even more of a problem was that Laurie outweighed Bebe by 15 pounds.

Bebe got onto her knees, fully aware that the ice was cracking around her. She yanked hard and made a little progress. "Laurie, try to stretch out! Then kick like you've never kicked before!"

The cold shock response had passed, and Laurie had her breathing under control. "I'm-I'm numb. I c-can't f-feel anything!"

"Keep kicking!" said Bebe, who had pulled Laurie halfway out. But then Bebe realized that Calvin had slipped under the surface. "Laurie, I'll get back to you in just a minute."

"No, I'll drown!"

"Let go of the branch. Keep your arms stretched out on the ice and get as much of your body out of the water as you can. I've got to save Calvin first!"

Taking her branch, Bebe crawled over to the other hole just as Calvin's head bobbed to the surface. "Take hold of the branch!" she ordered.

The boy was weak, shivering, and turning blue. He made a halfhearted attempt, but when she pulled, the branch slipped out of his hand. "Grab it, Calvin!" Before he could try again, the ice split open underneath Bebe and she plunged into the frigid water.

The shock from the bitterly cold water was so intense that it stole her breath. She couldn't even scream. Her body immediately began shaking and tightening her lungs, causing her to gasp for air. *Stay calm,* she told herself. *Get your breathing under control. You've got a few minutes before your body shuts down.* While she held on to the edge of the hole, she saw Calvin's eyes roll back and his head slide under the water. *He's lost consciousness!*

Bebe knew she had only a minute or two to get him out before he drowned — or for that matter, before they all did. To reach him meant letting go of the frozen edge of the hole. Her waterlogged clothes and the unbearable cold made it difficult to move. *I can't watch him die.* She let go and with two powerful strokes reached his body, which was now completely underwater. She hooked her arm around his neck and pulled him to the surface and then strained to reach the edge of the hole. Twice they went under and twice they resurfaced.

Bebe knew that thrashing in ice water causes the loss of body heat and energy, but she had to keep treading. Her heavy, soaked clothes were dragging her under so she couldn't float. Although her arms and legs were numb, she kept struggling and soon reached the edge of the hole. With one arm resting on the ice and the other around Calvin, she caught her breath. "Calvin!" she shouted. "Wake up!"

He blinked several times and then coughed. As he opened his eyes wider, he started to panic, pawing at her head.

"Calvin, climb up on me. Use me as a ladder so you can get out."

He gripped the collar of her jacket and pulled himself up. Then he clambered over her and flopped onto the ice. "Don't move!" she said.

The piercing cold hurt every muscle, joint, bone, and organ in Bebe's body. She was so cold that the pain burned. She was getting weaker by the second. *Stay calm. Find a way out.* She spotted a place on the edge of the hole where the ice was a little thicker. With great effort, she put herself into a horizontal position. Then she began kicking her legs as hard as she could and tried pulling herself up onto the ice. *Kick! Kick! Kick! I'm almost there!* But then the ice cracked and she sank back into the water. *Nooo!*

Bebe was losing strength. She knew she had one more chance before she would be too fatigued to escape on her own. *Isn't there anyone out there who can save us?* Once again, she placed her hands on top of the ice on the edge of the hole, stretched out, kicked, and tried pulling herself up. Her arms shaking wildly, she gave one last burst of kicking and, like a seal, scooted out of the water and onto the ice. *I did it! I did it!* For one brief moment, all the pain and cold went away as she basked in her success. Then her entire body shook with the cold creeps, a bitter reminder that her survival wasn't assured.

Afraid the ice would crack under her, Bebe began rolling, rather than crawling, away from the hole. "Calvin, do the same thing as I do," she said. Calvin did what he was told until he was able to get on all fours and crawl off the frozen pond.

Bebe worked her way over to Laurie. Barely conscious, the girl remained halfway out, draped over the edge of the ice hole, but from the waist down, her body was in the water. "I . . . can't . . . move," she muttered. "Don't . . . let me . . . die."

"I won't. I promise."

"Is . . . Calvin . . . dead?"

"No, he's safe." Bebe looked around. *Where is everybody?* "Help!" she shouted. "Help!" But in her weakened state, her voice didn't carry very far. Calvin was in no condition to get help. He was lying on the bank, shaking uncontrollably.

Her teeth chattering and her body shivering, Bebe wondered, *How am I going to get Laurie out? I wish I had a rope.* Searching the bank with her eyes, she spied a tree next to Calvin. A large, thick vine was dangling from it. *Maybe that will work.*

"Don't let go, Laurie. I'll be right back." Carefully, Bebe crawled to the bank where she tugged on the dead vine until a 20-foot section fell. On her way back, she checked on Calvin.

"C-c-cold," mumbled Calvin, his body shaking like an out-of-tune engine. He couldn't stop quivering. Neither could Bebe.

She returned to the ice hole where Laurie was starting to slip back into the water. While lying flat on the ice, Bebe fashioned a loop with the vine and shoved it over to Laurie. "Put it around you under your arms," Bebe said.

Laurie whined. "Can't."

"You must. If you don't, you'll go under and drown. You've got to do it!"

Whimpering and trembling, Laurie slowly managed to get the loop around her. But doing so caused her to slide back into the water until only her arms and head remained on the edge of the hole. Taking the other end of the vine, Bebe then crawled another few feet from the hole to where the DANGER! STAY OFF ~~THE ICE!~~ sign was posted. She stood up and, with her chest ~~pulling~~ on the vine, inch by inch, ~~until Laurie~~ was halfway out of the water.

But neither girl had any strength left. Bebe couldn't get Laurie out of the icy water. *She's going to die.* Bebe wrapped the vine around her forearm and slumped to her knees. *I've failed.* She closed her eyes and started to cry. *I'm . . . so tired . . . so cold. . . .*

Falling into a dreamlike state, she experienced a flurry of sensations — feeling freed from the strain of the vine, being carried in strong arms, getting wrapped in warm blankets, hearing wailing sirens and people speaking in worried voices.

When her eyes fluttered open, she saw her smiling, teary-eyed mother peering down at her. "Mommy? Where am I?"

"The hospital, sweetheart. The doctors say you're suffering from a severe case of hypothermia — the loss of body heat. Oh, what am I thinking. You already know what that means. I've been told you should make a full recovery. Isn't that wonderful? Oh, sweetheart, I heard what you did. I am so very, very proud of you."

It took Bebe a minute to remember the chilling details of the ordeal she had just endured. "And the others? Did they survive? Please tell me they're alive."

"Yes, sweetheart. Calvin has hypothermia, too. Laurie is in much worse shape. The doctors think it will take several weeks before she will be able to walk again because she's partially paralyzed from the waist down due to the intense cold. But they're hopeful she'll recover. Thank goodness a neighbor looked out the window and saw what was happening and called the fire department. They came ⬛⬛⬛⬛⬛⬛ very close to death. You and Calvin wouldn't ha⬛ ⬛⬛ much longer yourselves."

When the full story of Bebe's actions emerged, she was hailed as a hero. Kids at school looked at her differently than before, and were nicer to her. Oh, sure, they still groaned when she raised her hand every time the teacher asked a question that none of them could answer. But they also treated her with more respect, and she, in turn, became friendlier to them. She even offered to tutor the boy who stuck the LAUGH AT ME sign on her back.

The first time that Bebe saw Laurie in the hospital, Laurie croaked out a sheepish "hi."

Laurie's mother, Mrs. Robertson, hugged Bebe and said, "I can't begin to thank you for saving my children. Without you, they both would've drowned. You were so brave. And to think you risked your life after what they did to you." Turning to Laurie, Mrs. Robertson said, "Don't you have something to say to Bebe?"

Fighting back tears, Laurie said, "I'm really, really sorry for the way Calvin and I treated you. We were wrong. We shouldn't have been so mean and hit you with snowballs and called you names. I'm just glad you were there to save our lives."

"I'm glad we all survived," Bebe said.

"Tell me something, Bebe," said Mrs. Robertson. "I'm absolutely amazed by your actions. How did you know what to do?"

"A few weeks ago, I read a magazine article about how to save yourself if you fall through the ice," Bebe replied. "I remembered all the tips because, well, I am Little Miss Know-It-All."

THE CESSPOOL

The five boys wheeled their bicycles up to the construction site of a highway interchange. Pointing to a large culvert — a cement tube that went under the road — the group's leader, Billy Burton, exclaimed, "Wow, look at that. It's big enough for us to ride through. Let's do it!"

"I'm not so sure that's a good idea," said Kevin "Bones" Manoa. "What if there's a downpour and it fills up with . . ."

"Look at the sky, Bones. It's mostly blue. No big rain clouds," Billy said. Peering inside the culvert, he added, "It probably goes off at an angle, because I can't see any light at the other end. This is going to be fun. Bones, you go first."

"Me? Why me?" asked the 11-year-old who was tagged with the nickname for being so skinny.

"Because you're the only one who has a light on his bike."

"Well, I, um . . ."

"What's the matter, Bones? Are you afraid of the dark?"

"No, of course not!"

"Then go ahead and lead the way."

As the youngest and smallest of the group, Kevin had never been asked to lead anything with the group. The other four boys were older and in sixth or seventh grade. The fifth grader couldn't pass up the opportunity to go first, even though he hated confined, dark spaces. They gave him the willies ever since he and his mother were trapped in an elevator at an office building in downtown Honolulu after a power outage. Kevin, who was five at the time, and his mom had to sit in the pitch black for more than four hours. Kevin had kept a night-light on in his bedroom ever since.

Now he had to be the first one to enter a dark tunnel in front of his pals. He couldn't let them down. After all, when you wear glasses and braces and are underweight and short for your age, you need all the friends you can get. The last thing you want to do is prove that you're a weenie.

"Hey, Bones, are you chicken or what?" Billy snorted.

"Bawk! Bawk! Cluck! Cluck!" the other boys cracked, flapping their arms like chicken wings.

Kevin turned red, hopped on his bike, flicked on the headlamp and pedaled into the darkness. "Follow me — unless you're too scared!" he shouted over his shoulder. He got no more than twenty yards in when his heart began to race. His palms dripped with sweat and his body trembled, causing his bike to wobble just enough for the handlebars to scrape against the insides of the culvert.

The boys behind him were making scary sounds, and laughing as their voices echoed off the culvert's curved walls.

It's awfully dark in here, Kevin told himself. *Where does it end? Keep going. You can't chicken out now.* He had reached a turn in the culvert and suddenly his body relaxed. *Light! I see light at the end of the tunnel!* He pedaled faster and soon emerged at the other side.

When the others caught up with him, he said, "Whew! That was fun!" It really wasn't for him, although he felt a sense of accomplishment, having faced one of his fears and conquered it — at least for one day.

But Kevin would soon face this same fear again — only this time, it would be a matter of life or death.

Going back through the culvert wasn't as hard for Kevin. "Hey, guys, I have to go home now," he said after they came out. "I have to help my mom set up her booth at the Na Hula Festival." His mother, Lana, a native Polynesian, was proud of her culture and had passed down that appreciation to her son.

"Make sure to say hi to all the hula dancers," said Billy. Shaking his hips and moving his hands like a hula girl, Billy made the other boys laugh.

Kevin gave a fake grin and rode off along the north shore of Hawaii's Pearl Harbor toward his home in Pearl City. The harbor was the scene of the fierce Japanese attack in 1941 that had forced the United States to enter World War II. His route took him along streets shaded in palm trees and dotted with colorful bungalows.

On his way home, Kevin was thinking about all the desserts his mother was preparing to sell at the festival. He couldn't wait to get a bite of his favorite, Honolulu Lulu, made with crushed pineapple, whipped cream, shredded coconut, and cooked rice.

He snapped out of his mouthwatering daydream after hearing someone shout, "Suzu! Get back here!" Kevin looked to his right and saw a young Asian woman in a kimono chasing after a Yorkshire terrier. It was scampering across the front yard toward the street where a speeding pickup truck was approaching. Looking at the dog and then at the truck, Kevin estimated that the paths of the animal and vehicle would likely meet a few feet in front of him — unless he tried to stop it.

Kevin pulled to the curb, leaped off his bike and, with his arms outstretched, jumped up and down, trying to scare the dog away from the street. His actions worked. Without slowing down, the terrier made a sharp left and dashed into the neighbor's yard as the truck roared past.

"Suzu! Come here!" demanded the woman. "Suzu!"

The little dog wasn't paying any attention to her and instead was sniffing the neighbor's flowers. Kevin crawled up behind Suzu, then sprang on her, and caught her. The dog yelped in protest as Kevin brought the pet to its grateful owner.

"Oh, thank you so much," she said, cuddling Suzu. "You saved her life."

"I'm glad I could help," Kevin replied.

She bowed to Kevin. "I'm Mrs. Matsui, and you've already met Suzu." Coaxing a little boy, about two years old, who had been hiding behind her, she added, "And this is my son, Kisho. Suzu is not supposed to go outside, but Kisho opened the door and she bolted. I don't know who I should be mad at most — Kisho or Suzu."

Kisho waddled over to Kevin and held out his hand. In his

fist was a partially eaten Tootsie Roll. "Toots," the toddler said. "Toots."

"Oh, isn't that sweet?" said Mrs. Matsui. "Kisho wants to share his Tootsie Roll with you."

I don't want to share it with him, Kevin thought. *He's got slobber all over it. What am I going to do?* "No, thank you."

Kisho frowned. "Toots for you." He thrust out his hand again, so Kevin pretended to take a bite. "Mmm, good. Thank you."

But the toddler wasn't fooled and began to cry.

"Okay, okay," said Kevin. He took a bite and then choked it down. "Thank you, Kisho." *I hope I don't get sick from the kid's germs.* "Well, I better get home. I'm glad your dog is safe. Bye, Mrs. Matsui. Bye, Kisho." *You better not have any cooties.*

When Kevin returned home, he mentioned the Suzu incident to his mother. He didn't see the dog or Kisho or Mrs. Matsui for several months even though they lived only three blocks away from his house.

But they met again in a crisis that no one could have ever imagined.

It happened on the day when Kevin had helped his mother carry several plantings of tuberose bulbs to the home of Mrs. Ferguson, an elderly family friend and neighbor. While walking back, they watched an ambulance, two police squad cars, and three fire trucks pull up to a house at the end of the block. A crowd was gathering in the backyard. "Let's see what's going on," Kevin said.

When they reached the house, Kevin told his mother, "Hey, I know the people who live here — the Matsuis. You know, the ones whose dog I helped save." Kevin went up to a police officer

62

who was marking off the area with yellow tape and asked, "What's going on?"

"A little boy fell into a cesspool and he's stuck down there," the officer replied.

Kevin had heard his mother talk about cesspools recently after the local newspaper, the *Honolulu Advertiser*, ran a series on the dangers of these abandoned underground containers that are used for the disposal of human waste from toilets. One of the articles mentioned that although Hawaii was arguably the prettiest state in the union, it also was the cesspool capital of the nation. At the time, more abandoned cesspools existed in the Aloha State than anywhere else in the country.

And now a little boy was trapped at the bottom of one.

"No one can figure out how to get him out," a bystander said to the gathering crowd. "If they don't rescue him soon, he'll die from suffocation either from all the poisonous gases down there or lack of oxygen."

Firefighters, police, and paramedics were hustling back and forth. Kneeling next to the hole was Mrs. Matsui, wringing her hands close to her chest, her face a picture of agony. "My baby! My baby!" she wailed. Her grief-stricken husband was holding her for support.

From talking to the neighbors, Kevin learned that Kisho had been playing in the backyard with his parents and Suzu. He stood on top of the abandoned cesspool, which had been covered with wooden planks and nailed shut. When Kisho began jumping up and down on the boards, they snapped in two from rot. The boy plunged feetfirst down a narrow 15-foot-deep shaft and into a tank that contained a layer of disgusting human waste up to his chest. The only good news was that Kisho wasn't seriously injured from the fall. He was standing up in the foul muck and crying for his parents.

When the firefighters arrived, they ripped the rotten wood from the top of the cesspool, but the shaft was only 12 inches by 16 inches — much too small for any rescuer to enter. Emergency workers had taken a hose and connected it to an air tank. Then they dropped the hose down the shaft so the boy could breathe fresh air, and at least be kept alive, although no one knew for how long.

Kevin overheard officials discussing strategy. They decided against digging to make the shaft larger, fearing it would collapse and bury Kisho in debris. "We can get the drilling rig from the road construction crew at the new interchange and burrow a hole parallel to the shaft," said one of the rescuers. "Then we can dig a tunnel to the cesspool tank and bring him out that way."

"But that could take more than a day," said another rescuer. "The boy could die in the meantime from all the fumes."

"We'll keep pumping air down to him while we drill and hope for the best. There's no other way."

"Maybe we could lower someone in there and snatch the boy."

"We're all too big to fit in the shaft."

Maybe they're all too big, but I'm not, Kevin told himself. As he walked over to his mother, his heart began racing at the thought of what he was about to propose. *Should I really suggest it? Will they even let me? And if they do, can I really pull it off?*

"Mom," said Kevin, "Kisho could be stuck down there for over a day, and he might not survive. The best way to get him out is if someone small — someone like me — is lowered into the cesspool and pulls him out."

"Kevin, you can't be serious. It's much too dangerous."

"What if that were me down there, Mom, and some older boy offered to rescue me? Wouldn't you want his mother to give him permission?"

"Well, I guess so. . . ."

"Thanks, Mom." He took her hand and led her to the front of the cordoned-off area where he caught the attention of the fire captain who was in charge of the rescue operation.

"Excuse me, sir," Kevin said. "I'm Kevin Manoa and this is my mother, Lana. Before you drill, let me try to get Kisho. I'm small and skinny — my friends call me Bones — so I should be able to fit in the shaft."

The captain shook his head. "Son, thanks for the offer. But there's no way I'm going to risk your life. It's very hazardous. The noxious fumes in there could knock you out. The only reason the little boy is alive is because we're pumping air down in the cesspool."

"But I heard you say that Kisho could die — that the fumes will eventually get to him. And drilling will take another day to complete. Let me at least try."

The captain squinted at Kevin's mother. "And you approve of this?"

"I'm really worried for my son's safety," she replied. "But if there's a chance that he can help save that little boy's life, then I give my permission."

The captain studied Kevin's slender frame and bony arms. "Are you sure you're up to it, son?"

No, not really, Kevin thought. *What am I thinking?* "Y-y-yes, s-s-sir."

The captain put an arm around Kevin, hustled him over to the opening, and announced to the rescuers, "We're going to lower this young man in the hole and see if he can bring out Kisho."

Kevin glanced at the men and saw in their eyes a mix of respect for what he was about to do and doubt that he could actually rescue Kisho.

Mrs. Matsui, who was still at the edge of the opening, stood up and stared at Kevin. "I know you from somewhere."

"Yes, when your dog escaped."

"Of course!" She clasped his hand and bowed. "You're an angel sent here once again in a time of need."

The firefighters fitted Kevin with a rope sling that wrapped around the back of his thighs. Although it was an extremely warm day, Kevin felt a sudden chill. The thought of entering a dark, tight shaft made him shiver.

One worker who was adjusting the sling noticed Kevin's body shaking. "There's still time to back out," he whispered to Kevin.

"I'll be fine. I'm just a little scared, that's all."

"I understand. Keep in mind that you'll be in control while we're lowering you. If you feel like you can't go any farther because the shaft is too tight or the fumes are making you sick, just holler and we'll pull you right up."

Kevin nodded.

Mrs. Matsui dropped to her knees and yelled down in the hole, "Kisho, be brave. We're sending an angel down to get you!"

Kisho gave a little whimper.

"It's time," said the captain. "Are you ready, Kevin?" .

No, I'll never be ready for this. "Let's do it." Kevin sat on the edge of the hole and peered into the smelly darkness. "Uh, would you mind shining a light down there?" he asked. When the workers moved in a powerful work lamp, he clutched the rope, and then slid in feetfirst. It was an extremely tight fit. Even though he had to scrunch his scrawny shoulders, they still rubbed against the rough walls of the shaft.

As he was lowered, the stench from the cesspool grew stronger. And so did his fear of dark, tight spaces. He was shuddering and sweating, fighting off frightening thoughts of a cave-in that would bury him alive.

Oh, God, what am I doing in here, he thought. *Why did I volunteer for this?* His breathing came faster, but the more he inhaled, the more sick to his stomach he became from the nauseating fumes. *I want out of here! I can't stand the stench. I can't stand being here.* He closed his eyes but only for a moment.

"How are you doing, Kevin?" the captain shouted.

Kevin wanted to shout, "Pull me up, now!" But he didn't. "Okay, I guess." The fumes were making him woozy and he began to gag and cough. He felt like he was suffocating. "I-I don't know if I can make it. The fumes."

"Do you want us to pull you up?"

Yes! Yes! Yes! Just then, Kevin heard Kisho whine. *That poor little kid. I've gone this far. I've got to try.* "I'm so close, Captain. I can see Kisho. Keep lowering me."

A few seconds later, Kevin reached the foul-smelling muck and sank in up to his knees. For a moment, he thought he was going to pass out, but he grabbed the air hose and inhaled some of the fresh, pumped air. When he gained control of his senses, he saw how terrified Kisho was.

"Kisho, do you remember me? I was playing with your dog. You gave me a bite of your Tootsie Roll."

The boy nodded. "I want my mommy."

"I've come to take you out of here." Kevin looked up. The light at the top of the shaft seemed so far away. *Hurry up! No more talking.* Kevin gave the toddler a bear hug and said, "Hold on to me and I'll hold on to you." Then he shouted to the workers above, "We're ready! Take us up!"

Inch by inch they were raised out of the muck. Each held on tightly to the other. "Hurry up, hurry up," he muttered to the workers. About halfway to the top, where the shaft narrowed, they became lodged. "Stop! Stop!" he shouted. The rope was cutting into his thighs. "We're stuck!"

This was his worst nightmare. Fighting panic, Kevin squirmed and wiggled. So did Kisho until Kevin lost his grip on the boy and the toddler plunged back into the muck. "Oh, no! I lost him!" Looking down, Kevin shouted, "Kisho, say something."

The toddler responded by letting out a loud wail.

Kevin shouted to the workers, "Pull me up! Now!" Free from holding onto Kisho, Kevin was hauled up the shaft. Once he was lifted out of the hole, he collapsed on the ground and took several deep breaths of fresh air.

"Where's my baby?" screamed Mrs. Matsui. "Where's my baby?"

"He slipped out of my hands when we got stuck," Kevin replied.

Throwing her hands to the sides of her head, she buried her face in her husband's chest and sobbed. Her husband cried, too.

The captain came over to Kevin. "Can you try one more time?"

I really don't want to go down there, thought Kevin. But he looked over at the devastated parents and knew he had to try again. "I guess so, but the shaft is too narrow for the both of us."

"I have an idea that might work," said the captain. He tied a second rope around Kevin's waist. At the other end was a loop. "Put this loop under his armpits. Then, hold on to the rope so that when we pull you up, he will come up, too, right below you." The captain cocked his ear. "I don't hear Kisho crying anymore." He rushed over to the opening and shouted down, "Kisho! Kisho! Can you hear me?"

There was no answer.

Turning to Kevin, the captain said, "We have no time to lose. The boy might have passed out or slipped under the muck."

Oh, God, here we go again, thought Kevin. He was quickly lowered into the cesspool. It wasn't any easier the second time. In fact, it was worse and he began gagging. When he reached the muck, he found Kisho alive and standing up. But the toddler was in a daze.

69

Kevin quickly slipped the loop over the toddler's head until it was secured under his armpits. Then he held on to the rope. "Okay!" he shouted. "Get us out of here!"

The workers pulled on the sling and began lifting Kevin and Kisho out of the filth. It took less than a minute, much too slow for Kevin.

When they were lifted out, Kevin crawled a few feet away from the opening and threw up. Covered in mud and raw sewage, he reeked of a smell so horrible that no one wanted to get near him.

"Hose him down," the captain ordered a rescuer.

"Please," Kevin said. "I can't stand myself." He stood up while he was sprayed with a garden hose. Firefighters wrapped him in a blanket and took him to the hospital for observation. Kevin was released later that evening.

Meanwhile, paramedics gave Kisho oxygen before they stripped off his filthy, stinky clothes and gave him a quick bath. Kisho spent the night in the hospital and was sent home the next day with no health problems or injuries.

A day later, Kevin and his mother walked over to the Matsuis' to see how Kisho was feeling.

"You are an angel who saved my baby's life," said Mrs. Matsui, hugging Kevin.

"I'm glad things worked out," he said. "Sometimes it pays to be skinny like me."

Just then Kisho waddled over and held out a half-eaten Tootsie Roll. "Toots, Toots." Kevin sighed, kneeled down, and took a bite from the toddler's sticky fingers. *I sure hope he doesn't have cooties.*

DEAD MAN'S BRIDGE

Ever since she could remember, Angela Sluder loved the sound of trains. There was a certain comfort in knowing that no matter how hard and unsettling her life was, she could always count on the freight trains. Six times a day they rumbled on those old tracks behind her rickety four-room clapboard house outside a Missouri junction town. Six times a day the trains' wheels screeched, the railroad ties groaned, and the whistles blew — reminders to the 13-year-old that life goes on. Even the 11 P.M. freight train, which rattled the panes of her bedroom window and sometimes woke her up, provided Angela with an element of reliability, which was something she rarely found at home.

But then the rhythmic clangs, rattles, and jangles of the trains stopped bringing her any comfort — all because of that frightening close encounter on Dead Man's Bridge.

The 200-foot-long, single-track, steel trestle stretched over the St. Francis River 30 feet above the water. The bridge had no official name. However, according to local legend, a middle-aged man was fishing from the bridge years ago and had hooked a huge bass when a fast-moving freight train approached. He thought he had just enough time to reel in his big catch and get out of the way of the train. He was wrong. From then on the trestle was known as Dead Man's Bridge.

Over time, rust had turned the narrow bridge's triangular-shaped trusses a dirty reddish-brown. To most people, it was an ugly trestle. To kids, it was an exciting summertime amusement park, a perfect place to test their bravery . . . or stupidity. Sure, they knew jumping off the bridge was illegal and dangerous. But it was the height of summer, the water was cool, and leaping three stories off a bridge — especially if you could do a somersault on the way down — was an incredible rush. Besides, they were only doing what their fathers and grandfathers had done when they were kids, so the leapers were seldom, if ever, punished by their parents.

The bridge and the area around it weren't patrolled much, because it required a half-mile walk on a well-worn dirt path — the River Trail — from the nearest road to the trestle. Occasionally, a railroad cop would show up and threaten to arrest leapers and fence off the banks on either side of the bridge. But the kids kept playing there, anyway.

Angela never joined in the fun. And there was no way the kids would ever invite her. This was the early 1960s when white boys in the area ignored African-Americans — especially a shy, poverty-stricken girl like Angela.

Even if she wanted to play on the bridge, she couldn't. She

didn't have the time. Her mother, Bea, needed her, and so did her two younger sisters.

Angela's father, Lavelle, had recently abandoned them, not for the first — or the last — time. It seemed that whenever the weather turned nice, Lavelle would pick a fight with Bea and use it as an excuse to leave. He'd hop on a freight train — usually the 11 P.M. out of St. Louis — and wouldn't show up for a month or two. Sometimes he'd return with a wad of twenty-dollar bills and treat "my favorite girls" to a nice dinner at Mister Steak. Too often, however, he came back with only a few coins in his pocket.

Bea was a seamstress — some said the best in town — who altered dresses, skirts, pants, and suits for those who could afford it. She earned barely enough to meet the basic needs of the family. It sure didn't help when Lavelle, a handyman, went off on one of his outings. Bea also took in ironing to earn a few extra bucks.

Lately, with the car not running and Lavelle gone, Angela had to pick up and deliver the items that needed sewing or ironing. It meant walking as much as four miles roundtrip, carrying a basket of clothing. The summer was especially busy for Angela. During her pickups and deliveries, it didn't take long for her short, chubby arms and legs to glisten with sweat. Her plaid cotton dress would be soaked by the time she made it home.

One day, Angela picked up a large load of clothes that needed ironing. She put the basket on her head, thinking it would be easier than carrying it on her hip. She had seen magazine pictures of beautiful African women in colorful garb balancing large loads on their heads, and she figured she could do it, too. It wasn't as easy as it looked, and twice she spilled all the contents on the sidewalk. But she eventually got the hang of it.

While returning home with the basket on her head, she took the shortcut — the River Trail, which snaked along the top of the high riverbank by Dead Man's Bridge. As expected, she saw kids leaping off the trestle and dangling from the rope swing. Four boys were gathered at the near end of the bridge about ten yards from the dirt path that Angela was using.

Usually the boys paid no attention to her, but on this day she sensed that all eyes were on her. She quickened her pace and stepped over the rails of the single railroad track. Just then she heard *plink*, and then another *plink*, and another. She felt a pebble hit her leg, and a larger stone strike her in the back. She turned around and saw the boys lobbing stones at her.

"Hey, wait. Stay still for a second!" one of the boys shouted at her, giving her a friendly wave. He was Will Talbot. She recognized the 15-year-old because his mother was a customer of her mother's. She smiled at him, thinking maybe he would apologize for his friends' behavior. "We're trying to score a basket!"

Humiliated that the boys were using her as a human basketball hoop, Angela scurried out of range of the stone tossers. *I wish a train would come along and slam into . . . No, I can't think like that. I guess they can't help being jerks. They're boys.*

About a half mile away, Angela reached another set of tracks and followed them toward home. She carefully walked between the wooden ties to avoid the creosote — a brownish, oily preservative — that oozed out of the ties in the heat. Walking on the crushed rock between the ties and rails was better than hiking outside the tracks, because the railway bed was lined with thorny brambles and stickers.

Angela knew it wasn't safe to walk along the tracks like this. She lost count of the number of times her father had lectured her and her sisters about the dangers. "Trains go really, really fast," he told them. "You might not realize it, but they can be pretty quiet, especially if the wind is right or there's a bend in the tracks, and you're not paying attention. Respect the tracks. Don't walk between the rails. You might fall and hurt yourself just as a train approaches and then . . ." He'd slap his hands. "You're dead."

That night, Angela couldn't sleep. It was stiflingly hot, and the bed she shared with her sisters seemed too crowded. She went out onto the porch, hoping to catch a little breeze. There was none.

In the distance, she heard the train whistle its approach to a crossing — the 11 P.M. from St. Louis. In less than two minutes, it would rumble by the house on its way west. So many times she fantasized about hopping aboard and riding the rails to a new life — a life where she lived in a new house, shopped for new store-bought clothes, and made new friends who didn't care about the color of her skin.

She was pretty sure it was the same train that her dad had taken, although he didn't catch it near the house because the freight went too fast at that point. But about two miles away, it slowed down for a sharp bend. That's where he'd hop on.

Angela pictured herself running alongside the brown boxcars

as they slowed down just for her. She'd catch hold of a handle, pull herself up, and climb to the roof of a boxcar. Then she'd watch her hardscrabble life disappear into the night. *I wonder if that's what Daddy feels every time he hops a freight — a way to escape from all this,* she thought.

She lay down on the porch swing and let the clickety-clack rhythm of the passing train lull her asleep. It would be the last time those railroad sounds would give her a feeling of comfort.

The next morning, Angela made a delivery of ironing to Mrs. Bartlett, taking the long way to avoid going past the boys of Dead Man's Bridge. On her return, the skies darkened and it looked like rain soon, so she took the River Trail. As she neared the trestle, she didn't see any kids jumping off. *Good,* she thought. *They're not here. Maybe this will be my lucky day.*

When she reached the tracks, she looked both ways because she knew the 3:45 freight was due anytime. Gazing down the length of the trestle, she gasped. A boy and a girl — they couldn't have been more than five or six — were sitting in the middle of the bridge in between the rails, tossing rocks in the air. *They look familiar,* she thought. *I think they're Mrs. Talbot's kids.* She looked around. *Why are there no adults or older children nearby?*

Just then she heard the 3:45's horn blow. She knew the train would be approaching from the other end of the trestle in less than a minute.

"Get off the bridge!" she yelled to the children. "A train is coming! Hurry!"

Either the children didn't understand her or ignored her,

because they didn't get up. *They'll be killed,* she thought. *I've got to get them out of there.*

She dashed toward the middle of the trestle, all the while yelling at the kids and waving her arms. "Get off the bridge! A train is coming! Get off!"

The kids stood up, stared at her, and then backed away. *They act like they're afraid of me. Is it because I'm black?* "Don't run away," she yelled at them. "I'm Angela. I pick up your mama's clothes for ironing and mending. Remember me?"

The kids stopped and nodded.

"Come to me, please. A train will be here in a few seconds. We have to get off the bridge right now."

The horn sounded louder. The engine had rounded the bend and was approaching the trestle. Seeing the train, the boy began running toward Angela. But the girl stood motionless. She was paralyzed by fear.

Angela was about twenty yards away from her. *If I don't rescue her, the train will hit her,* Angela thought. As the boy sprinted past her, Angela raced to the girl and scooped her up. Then she wheeled around and hurried toward the near end of the bridge, hoping they could reach it before the train did.

The engine was closing in on the trestle. Angela looked back. "We're going to make it," she said.

But then about ten yards from the end of the bridge, the boy fell and cried out in pain.

"Get up!" shouted Angela. "Get up!"

He struggled to his feet but fell again. "I can't. I hurt my ankle. Help me!"

The engineer was frantically blowing the horn. Angela could tell by the length of the blasts that he saw them and was trying to stop. The train's brakes were engaged, causing a horrible screeching sound. But she knew that a heavy freight train like the 3:45, pulling about 60 to 80 cars, would need at least half a mile to stop.

Seconds. That's all they had left.

With the girl under one arm, Angela yanked on the boy's hand and pulled him to his feet. "Put your arm around me," she ordered. He did what he was told and, using Angela for support, began hobbling.

There's no way we can make it off the bridge in time, Angela thought. She knew there wasn't enough room on the narrow trestle for them to stand on the side as the train went by. "Trains overhang the rails by three feet on either side," Lavelle had told Angela. "If you're dumb enough to stand next to the tracks, consider this: Things like metal straps and chains occasionally break during shipment and hang off the sides of freight cars. How do you think it would feel to be slapped in the face with a chain or metal strap moving at fifty miles an hour? And even if everything was strapped down, you have to understand that a fast-moving train can create a suction that draws you under its wheels. So keep far away from the tracks."

The train was bearing down on Angela and the two kids. They were seconds away from death. There was no escape for them — except one. They had to jump.

"Do you know how to swim?" she asked them.

"No," they answered in unison.

"Neither do I."

The train was now only fifty feet away, unable to stop.

Angela turned the children toward the side so they faced the river, and together they stepped over a girder. When she looked at the water 30 feet below, she hesitated. From this angle, the bridge seemed so much higher than it did from the trail. "Hold your breath!"

"Noooo!" they screamed and began to fight her.

The squealing, braking train was virtually on top of them. Clutching a hand of each child, Angela closed her eyes and leaped off the bridge, towing them with her just as the freight train thundered past them.

The kids shrieked all the way down before they slammed into the river feetfirst. Plunging under the water, Angela opened her eyes and saw nothing but bubbles and foam swirling around her. *Get to the surface!* Angela thought.

Still holding the kids, she began kicking frantically until her head broke the surface. She gulped air and then pulled up the kids. They were gagging and crying and spitting out water.

"Kick!" she yelled. "Kick! And take a breath and hold it!"

She slipped under the water and struggled to resurface for another quick gulp. The squirming kids were dragging her down. She knew she had a better chance of surviving if she let go of them. But she couldn't do that, because as nonswimmers they would likely drown. The current in the river had pushed them downstream under the bridge. Every chance she had, she yelled "Help!", then took a deep breath and held it. At no time did Angela panic. She was too busy trying to save her life and the lives of the two children. "Help!"

But the little girl stopped thrashing and closed her eyes. *Oh, no! She's passed out,* Angela thought. *I've got to keep her head above water.* But the harder Angela tried to help the little girl, the more they kept slipping under the water. The terrified boy then latched onto Angela's neck, choking her and making it impossible for any of them to reach the surface.

Angela felt a tug and lost her grip on the little girl. *She's gone!* Angela thought. *I've lost her for good.*

Weary and scared, Angela had used up all her energy in her fight to survive. *I can't hold out any longer. I wonder what it's like to drown.* She was ready to give up. *I tried to save them. I really tried.*

Just then, she felt a strong hand seize her under her arm, pull her and the boy to the surface, and lug them close to shore. When she finally reached the shallow water, she stood up on wobbly legs and sucked in air. *I didn't drown after all! But how did that happen?* Exhausted and shaky, Angela stumbled to the bank where she saw Will Talbot trying to resuscitate his little sister. Next to them was their younger brother, kneeling on the sandy bank, sobbing and coughing.

Moments later the little girl spit up water and began to wail.

"Thank God!" Will cried out, hugging his sister. "I'm so, so sorry, Sally. It's all my fault. I never should have left you and Donny out of my sight."

Breathing heavily, Angela went over to Will and said, "Was that you who pulled me toward the bank?"

"Yeah," he replied, brushing sand off Sally's face.

"Thank you."

"I saw what happened," he said. "You saved Donny's and Sally's lives."

"What were they doing on the bridge?"

"I was babysitting them, and I took them to Dead Man's Bridge because they wanted to see it. We had just left when I bumped into some friends. While I was talking to them, the kids took off and ran back to the bridge. When my friends left, I couldn't find Donny and Sally. Then the train came. They would have been killed if it hadn't been for you."

For the first time he looked her in the eyes and said, "I don't even know your name."

"It's Angela. Angela Sluder — the girl who delivers ironing to your mama, the girl who you and your buddies were throwing rocks at."

Will cringed and looked down at his feet. "Yeah. I'm sorry about that."

She nodded in acceptance. *Imagine, a white boy apologizing to a black girl,* she thought. *And I helped save two lives. I guess this really is my lucky day.*

THE BALL
OF FIRE

Chad McCracken wasn't sure what to expect at school on his first day back after the accident. *Will they make fun of the way I look?* wondered the freshman. *Will they stare at me or refuse to look at me? Will they think I'm a freak?*

As the car he was riding in pulled up in front of Arrington High, he said, "Mom, I'm not sure I'm ready yet."

"I know you're feeling a little uneasy right now. But things will go better than you think," she said soothingly.

"Easy for you to say. Your face isn't scarred with burn marks that make you look like an alien."

"It's true you have a few scars. But you still have those big brown eyes, that winning smile, and a personality that makes everybody like you the minute they see you. Chad, you'll do fine. You better get going or you'll be late for class."

It's better if I'm late, he thought. *Then I won't have to face seeing everyone in the hall.*

Five months of recovering from second- and third-degree burns on his face and arms had eroded Chad's confidence. He went through more than a dozen operations and would need many more before he would be satisfied with his appearance. In the few times he was out in public since the accident, he encountered the pointing, whispering, and blatant stares of insensitive people. He put up with those who walked past him in the mall, then turned and walked backward just so they could gape a few seconds longer.

The endless skin grafts, doctor visits, and medications had stripped him of his very identity — at least in his mind — as a football player, a jock, and a dude. The burn injuries meant he couldn't play any sports during the year, and the scars on his face and arms didn't make him feel good about himself.

He was fretting because although this was his first day of high school, it was the second semester for everyone else. He opened the door to the car, stepped out, and hesitated.

"Do you want me to go in with you?" his mother asked.

"Mom, please. It's bad enough that I'm a freak. Having my mother escort me into school would for sure make me the laughingstock of Arrington High."

He pulled his baseball cap down over his eyes until the bill touched the top edge of his sunglasses, and he plodded toward the entrance. His stomach was twisted in knots. His hands felt clammy.

Come on, he told himself. *Get a grip on yourself. I'm not just a burn victim. I'm a person named Chad McCracken. No matter what reaction I get from them, I'll get through this. I hope.*

During his personal pep talk, never once did he regret the decision that caused him to suffer those horrible burns.

"The Giants are down by five, and there's time for one more play," Chad hollered. Clutching the football in his hands, he said, "The clock is ticking toward zero." He backpedaled. "McCracken takes the snap and drops back." He ducked and dodged several imaginary linemen. "He's running for his life. Oh . . . oh . . . he sees David Anders streaking down the sidelines." Chad heaved the ball toward his best friend who was running across his sprawling front yard about 20 yards away. "McCracken spots Anders and fires a long pass . . ." David made a fingertip catch. . . ."Touchdown! The New York Giants beat the Dallas Cowboys on the final play of the game!"

Chad and David ran toward each other, leaped up, and bumped chests in celebration.

"Great catch, Davey!"

"Great throw, Chad!"

The two had been tossing the football back and forth for more than an hour, talking about their anticipation of the first day of practice for the freshman team. Chad and David had been best buds since fourth grade and had played together on many sports teams for years. Now they were about to enter high school together. Even though class didn't officially start for two weeks, football tryouts were slated for next week. They both were tall for their age, but Chad was about twenty pounds heavier and more muscular than his friend.

"With your weight and size, don't you think you'd make a great defensive end or linebacker?" David asked.

"Nah, I want to play quarterback."

"Hey, that's the position I'm going for."

"But I have the strongest arm."

"And the biggest head."

Chad playfully shoved David, who began to retaliate, but stopped after hearing a loud bang that came from the normally quiet Virginia country road that fronted David's yard. The boys turned their heads in time to see a semi pulling a tanker full of gasoline. It was an odd sight because seldom did a tractor trailer ever use the road. Their surprise turned to alarm when they realized the tanker had blown its left rear tire as it entered the sharp right curve on the east side of David's property. In slow motion, the tanker began to tilt to the left, and the blown tire started smoking. The back end tipped even more, causing the semi to lose control.

Chad and David could see the driver furiously trying to regain control, but the tanker kept teetering until another tire on the left side exploded. "That truck is going to flip over!" Chad declared. As soon as he blurted out the words, the tanker did just that, screeching and sliding on its left side with all its wheels off the pavement. Because it was still connected to the semi, the tanker yanked the cab onto its left side, too, with the passenger-side door facing skyward.

"I can't believe what I'm seeing!" David shouted.

"Call nine-one-one!" Chad ordered. "I'll see if the driver is hurt."

As he started to run toward the wreck, Chad hadn't processed David's words of warning: "Don't get too close. It could explode." When Chad reached the cab, he noticed the engine was still running, and the tanker was making an ominous hissing sound. He started to back away, but then he heard moaning coming from inside the cab.

Chad inched forward again until he was in front of the cab. Through the cracked windshield he saw the trucker slumped against the driver-side door, which was resting on the pavement. "Are you hurt?" Chad shouted.

"Yes," the driver groaned. "My shoulder and legs."

"Don't worry. I'll get you out of there." Chad climbed up the chassis until he was on top of the overturned cab. He tugged at the passenger-side door, and discovered it was locked. He tried kicking it, but had little luck with his tennis shoes.

David and his mother burst out of the house and ran toward the wreck. They stopped about 50 feet away.

"Davey, come on and help me!" Chad shouted. "And bring me a rock!"

David started to break for the tanker, but his mother held him by the arm. "No, it's too dangerous!" she warned. "Stay here!"

Pointing to the rear of the tanker, David yelled to Chad, "The truck is on fire. You have to get out of there!"

"Not until I get this guy out! I need a rock. Throw one up to me!"

David found a baseball-sized rock and hurled it up to Chad who used it to smash open the passenger-side window. Then he reached in, unlocked the door, and opened it. "Can you move at all?" he asked the driver, who was folded over the steering wheel.

The trucker, a bearded, long-haired man in his twenties,

squirmed. "A little." Blood trickled down his face, and he closed his eyes.

"Hurry, Chad!" David shouted from outside. "The fire is getting bigger. This rig is going to explode any second!"

Chad didn't hesitate and lowered himself into the cab until his legs straddled the semiconscious man. "I need you to stand up," Chad told him. "Can you do that?"

The bleeding driver, his eyes half shut, nodded. Chad got him to his feet and propped him against the dashboard. "Don't move." Chad climbed out the open passenger-side door. Then he reached back and pulled the driver out. Putting him over his shoulder, Chad worked his way down the chassis until they reached the pavement.

"Henry," muttered the driver. "Where's Henry?"

"There's someone else in the cab?"

"Henry," the man mumbled.

"Who's Henry?"

The driver didn't answer. He had lost consciousness and slumped to the ground just as David arrived.

"I think there's someone else in the sleeper compartment of the cab," Chad said. "Davey, get the driver out of here. I'm going back in."

"Don't do it, man. Look at the flames. This thing is about to blow."

"Go! Go!" Chad urged.

As David was dragging the unconscious driver away, he pleaded with Chad one more time. "Come with me, please."

David's mother screamed, "Chad, get away from there!"

But Chad paid no attention and charged back to the wreck, climbed the chassis, and scrambled into the cab. "Henry! Henry! Are you in here?" he shouted. He peered into the sleeper behind the cab but didn't see anyone. He was turning away when he heard, "Oh, boy!" *Squawk!* "Oh, boy!"

Chad spotted a large parrot shivering in the far corner. "You're Henry?"

"Henry!" *Squawk!* "Henry!"

"I'm risking my life to save a parrot?"

Chad lunged for the frightened bird and grabbed it. In protest, Henry pecked at Chad's hands, but the teen ignored the bites. At the open passenger-side door, he tossed the bird into the air. Henry, whose wings had been clipped, fluttered to the ground and then hopped away from the wreck.

The whines from police and fire-engine sirens grew louder as Chad jumped down from the truck. *Good. They're coming just in time*, he thought. But the moment his feet landed on the pavement, one of the fuel tanks directly behind the cab exploded, launching flames 15 feet into the air. The force from the blast knocked Chad down, stunning him. Before he could scramble to his feet, burning gasoline rained down on him, igniting his clothing and singeing his hair.

At first the pain felt like the time he was attacked by a swarm of yellow jackets. But this was much worse. He held his bare arms up in front of him, unable to comprehend that they were on fire. He could hardly breathe because the ball of fire had stolen most of the oxygen around him.

I don't want to die this way, he told himself. *I can't die, not like this.* Staggering to his feet, Chad ripped off his burning

T-shirt and used his hands to smother his smoldering, fuel-soaked hair. He wasn't aware that the back of his jeans were on fire.

Dazed and in shock, he stumbled away from the fiery wreck, but everything seemed too sluggish, too quiet, too out of focus. He spotted David and Mrs. Anders looking at him in horror. He saw bystanders in the yard, pointing at him with pity and anguish. Off to his right, he noticed that the volunteer firefighters had arrived and were leaping off their trucks. He spotted sheriff's deputies and emergency workers hovering over the injured driver. In his clouded state of mind, everyone was hustling but he saw them in slow motion; everyone was shouting but he heard nothing.

When he reached the grass, Chad, who now felt the pain from his flaming pants, fell to the ground and rolled around until a firefighter stopped him and wrapped him in a special blanket. Suddenly his senses were overloaded with the sounds of shouts and sirens; the smells of burning fuel and rubber; the feelings of heat and pain. Lots of pain.

"Everything is going to be okay," the firefighter said. "We're going to get you to the . . ."

Ka-BOOM! The entire tanker, which was holding 7,500 gallons of gasoline, exploded with such force that the ground shook and flames soared 50 feet high. The earsplitting blast superheated the air, causing onlookers to scream and run for cover. The firefighters pulled Chad and the driver farther away from the wreck and then aimed streams of water on the blazing wreckage.

Chad felt his skin curling up like a piece of paper on fire.

Paramedics put an intravenous needle in him and placed him on a gurney (a stretcher on wheels). He looked up and saw David staring at him. David forced a smile in a weak attempt to mask his shock at seeing his burned pal.

"I look pretty bad, huh, Davey?"

"Uh, um. No, man. Well, you do kind of look like you spent a few hours too long in the tanning booth."

"I guess I'm going to miss the tryouts."

"You'll be on the football field in no time."

"What about the driver?"

"He's banged up pretty bad. The ambulance took him away."

"And that stupid bird?"

"My mom has it."

As the paramedics rolled Chad across the yard, each bump felt like a hundred needles stabbing him in his back. David was hustling alongside him. "Chad, I'm sorry I didn't go into the cab with you. It's just that the flames were getting closer and . . ."

"It's okay, Davey. You did what you had to do, and I did what I had to do."

Hearing the hospital helicopter landing nearby, he told David, "At least one good thing came out of this."

"What could that possibly be?"

"I'm about to take my first helicopter ride." By the time the chopper was airborne, Chad had passed out.

Doctors determined that Chad suffered first-, second-, and third-degree burns over much of his face, arms, and back. First-degree burns cause some damage to the outer layer of skin, called the epidermis. Second-degree burns damage the epidermis, peeling away layers of flesh and exposing nerve endings. Though not as severe as third-degree burns, these are often the most painful of all because nerve endings are uncovered. Third-degree burns go all the way through the seven layers of skin. Oil and sweat glands and hair follicles are burned away. Because nerve endings are destroyed, these burns are less painful than second-degree ones. However, the skin is so badly damaged that it cannot heal on its own. The dead tissue must be removed quickly because it is a breeding ground for bacteria. Treatment requires skin grafts.

In Chad's case, skin was taken from unburned areas of his body to cover the severely burned sections. He lost about 20 percent of his skin to burns and grafts. He had to sleep with his arms in suspended splints and underwent painful physical therapy every day. For a time, much of his body was covered in a special wrap that made him look like a mummy.

After a week of feeling sorry for himself, Chad made up his mind that he would get through this recovery. He relied on his faith and a strong belief in the power of positive thinking. And no regrets. *I'd do the same thing again,* he told himself.

But it wasn't easy. Healing from a burn injury is painfully slow and measured in months and years rather than days and weeks. Some days were worse than others; some were better.

One of the better ones in the hospital occurred when Chad had a special visitor two weeks after the accident. Leaning on a cane, a clean-shaven, ponytailed man in his twenties limped into the room and sat in a chair by Chad's bed.

"Remember me?" the man said. "I'm Tom Sellers, the driver of the tanker. You saved my life."

Chad nodded. "You look a lot better than when I last saw you."

"Yeah. Concussion, broken collar bone, broken leg. But I'm doing fine now. How are you feeling?"

"Hot, itchy, dry, raw. And I hurt, too. But otherwise, okay."

"I'm so sorry the accident has caused you all this pain and suffering."

"It wasn't your fault."

"I still feel bad. If only I hadn't gotten lost, I wouldn't have been on that road. If only I hadn't brought along Henry, none of this would have happened to you."

Boy, isn't that the truth? thought Chad, closing his eyes. *If only I hadn't gone over to Davey's that day. If only the tire hadn't blown. If only the driver hadn't mentioned Henry's name.* Chad shook his head in an effort to dump those thoughts from his brain. *Forget all the "if onlys." It won't take you to anywhere but misery.*

"So, how is that bird of yours?" Chad asked.

"Okay, I guess. He doesn't talk as much as he used to, and he's been pulling out his feathers from time to time. I guess he has what the doctors describe as posttraumatic stress syndrome."

"Well, at least he's alive."

"Yes, like me." Tom cleared his throat. "I'm not good with words, and sometimes I get all balled up when I try to speak from the heart, but here goes: I would have burned to death if it hadn't been for you. My wife would have been a widow at the age of twenty-three and our unborn son — he's due in a couple of months — would be entering this world without a daddy.

"Chad, what you did — risking your life to save a complete stranger — is the bravest, greatest, most wonderful thing that one human being can do for another. I know you've paid an awfully high price for your heroism — a price that I can never repay in full. But I'd like to try.

"My wife, Molly, and I talked it over. And we want to honor you in a very special way." Tears welled up in Tom's eyes, and his voice cracked. "When our son is born, we're going to name him Chad, after you."

Not the emotional type, and uncomfortable in sensitive situations, Chad tried to make light of the moment. "Wow, that's pretty cool. It's a good thing my name isn't Humpersnickerfloodle."

But the magnitude of his heroism and the physical and mental toll from his injuries surfaced all at once. Chad began to cry, softly at first before erupting into a full-blown sob. Tom wept with him.

Like all burn victims, Chad wanted the burns to heal, the pain to go away, the scars to disappear. He wanted the itching to stop and the repeated nightmares of that fateful day to end. He wanted his former life back. He wanted to be "normal" again. Right now.

Fortunately, the love and support of his family and friends helped Chad during the rough times. David stopped by the hospital every day until football practice started. Then he saw his friend on the weekends. During one such visit, David seemed edgy and wasn't his usual funny self.

"What's with you today?" asked Chad.

"Chad, I need your forgiveness."

"Okay. I forgive you for dropping all those perfect passes I threw."

"C'mon, man. I'm serious. I should have been right behind

you when you rescued that driver. I just didn't have the courage you did."

"I got to him first because I'm faster than you."

"Chad, please, this is hard for me. I feel so guilty."

"What did you do that was wrong? You called nine-one-one, you threw me a rock so I could break the window and, after I got him out, you dragged the driver away before the truck exploded."

"The rescue would have gone faster had I gone in the cab with you. It's just that when I saw the flames . . ."

"Look, Davey, I'm not going to forgive you, because there's nothing to forgive. You knew the risks and made a choice. So did I. And I got burned. Just let it go."

"There's something else. I was named the starting quarterback on the freshman team. Let's face it, Chad. If this accident hadn't happened, you'd be the one taking the snaps behind center, not me."

"Well, enjoy it now, my friend, because next year, that job is mine." Chad said it with a smile — but he meant it.

Chad hurdled over many obstacles throughout his lengthy recovery while missing the first semester of his freshman year. Now he was about to face his latest challenge — returning to class with a face that was still scarred. He felt conflicted. He wanted to get on with his high school life, but he was afraid that fellow students would treat him either as a freak to ridicule or a victim to pity.

After his mother dropped him off on his first day, Chad waited until the bell sounded so the halls would be empty. He went to the office to make sure his registration was in order.

He was surprised that the staff treated him nicely — no silent gasps, no turning away, no staring.

Yeah, but those are adults, he thought. *Kids are different.* As he walked to his first class, he was so nervous he could barely swallow, and his legs felt like Jell-O. He stopped a few feet from the class door. In his mind, he went through the possible reactions of his classmates: *They snicker at me. They gasp at my scarred face. They show fake sympathy. They ignore me — no, that's not going to happen. There'll be some sort of a reaction. Well, here goes.*

He opened the door and stepped into the room. The teacher stopped talking to the class as everyone turned to Chad. He froze for a moment, scanning the room for a vacant desk that he could scurry to. But before he could take a step, someone clapped. Then others clapped. Soon the entire room echoed with applause as every student stood up and gave Chad an ovation.

It's good to be back in school, he thought.

THE TOWER OF TERROR

Brooke Bailey was walking home from school when she heard a child giggle. She looked around but didn't see anyone.

"Hee-hee."

She cocked her ear and twirled around, her long black hair flowing like a cape. The voice was coming from above. She looked up at a leafy oak tree and saw two bare legs swinging back and forth. "Corey Shearson, is that you?"

"Uh-huh. Corey."

The eighth grader dropped her book bag and ran to the trunk of the tree. She figured that Corey, a mentally challenged ten-year-old neighbor, had sneaked out of the house again. "Oh, dear, you shouldn't be up in a tree. You could get hurt."

She shinned up the oak and sat on a large branch across from Corey about 10 feet off the ground. "What are you doing up here?" she asked.

He shrugged his shoulders.

"Can I help you down?"

Corey started to whine. "Scared."

"Hold on to me and we'll go down together, okay?" Slowly she reached out to him, but he jerked back and lost his balance. "Corey! No!" She lunged for him but it was too late. He fell out of the tree, landed on his feet, tumbled to the ground, and rolled on his right shoulder.

Brooke slid down and ran over to him. "Are you hurt?" she asked.

He looked at her and frowned. He pushed her away and limped back into his house. She followed him and rang the doorbell. When his mother answered, Brooke explained what had happened.

"This seems to be his latest thing," Mrs. Shearson explained. "Whenever he thinks he's done something wrong, he goes and finds some place high to hide. Last week, he accidentally broke a dish and we found him sulking on the windowsill in the attic. Today, he spilled chocolate milk on the cat, and while I was cleaning up the mess, he slipped out of the house and climbed the tree. Thank goodness he wasn't hurt. Brooke, it was so thoughtful of you to try to help him."

The next time Brooke saw Corey was several months later — on an incredibly nerve-racking morning that nearly claimed his life.

Growing up in West Virginia's Cumberland Plateau, Brooke was a busy girl. She played in the school band — she was second-chair clarinet — wrote a column for the monthly school newspaper, and ran long distance on the track team.

One spring day, she planned to jog the three miles home after school. She wanted to get in shape for track season, which would begin in a few weeks. After changing into her running shoes and shorts, she stuffed her school clothes in her book bag. Fortunately, she didn't have much homework for the weekend, so her bag wasn't too heavy.

Brooke ran along the shoulder of Mulford Road, a hilly and curvy country lane that weaved through a narrow valley of timberland and a few chicken farms. She chose this route because few cars used the road.

Striding gracefully on her long, thin legs, Brooke didn't push herself. She kept a steady pace. About halfway through her run, she headed up a hill when she heard a car on the other side skid and strike something metallic. Brooke broke into a sprint until she reached the crest of the hill and saw the accident. A car that had been heading in her direction had spun out of control and plowed through a fence that surrounded a tall electrical transmission tower.

Brooke rushed to the scene and was surprised to discover that the driver was Mrs. Shearson. The woman, who wasn't hurt, was examining the car's damaged front end while Corey sat on the ground, his arms wrapped around his knees. He was rocking back and forth.

"Mrs. Shearson, are you hurt?" Brooke asked. "Is Corey hurt?"

"We're not injured, just shaken up," replied Mrs. Shearson.

"What happened?"

"Oh, Corey was having one of his episodes. I was taking him to the farm of a friend of mine so he could see the new colt that was born last week. He loves horses. But something set him off, and he became quite angry in the backseat. I think his lunch box came open and spilled. He took off his seat belt, and when I told him to put it back on, he started tugging on my hair. I lost control of the car and ran off the road and knocked down the fence. Wouldn't you know, the nearest house is about a half mile away from here?"

"I was jogging home anyway, so why don't you stay here and I'll run up ahead and send some help. Should I call Mr. Shearson?"

"Yes, dear, that would be nice." Mrs. Shearson wrote the number down on a piece of paper. "And please call McAllister's Towing. They're in the phone book."

"Will Corey be all right?"

The boy was still rocking back and forth, mumbling to himself.

"Yes, it was pretty frightening for him. I think he feels badly for causing the accident. I'd better go comfort him."

Brooke ran to the nearest house where an elderly woman let her use the phone. The woman then drove Brooke back to the accident scene, and together they waited for Mr. Shearson and the tow truck to arrive.

During the wait, Mrs. Shearson told Brooke, "Corey won't have anything to do with me. He's pretty upset."

"Can I try?"

Mrs. Shearson nodded.

Brooke went over to Corey, who was still sitting on the ground. When she gently touched his shoulder, he swatted her hand away. "Corey, I'm glad you and your mom didn't get hurt. Would you like a drink of water? I have some in my book bag."

He shook his head. "Corey bad. Mommy mad."

"It was an accident. And your mommy isn't mad at you. She's upset because . . ."

"Go away!" He buried his head under his arms.

I hope you don't plan on climbing another tree again, thought Brooke, remembering how Corey often reacted when he felt he had done something wrong.

When Brooke came home late, she told her worried mother what had happened at the tower.

"It's a shame, but Corey is getting more difficult to handle," her mother said. "I heard the Shearsons are thinking of putting him into a special home that can better deal with mentally challenged children. He'd stay there during the week and come home on weekends."

"I feel sad for him and his family," Brooke said. "It must be so hard on everyone."

"I'm sure they love him very much, but for his own safety, they might not have any choice but to put him in a facility. Apparently, he's run off more than once and had a few violent episodes. But other times, he's the sweetest child in the neighborhood."

"What a difficult decision it must be for the Shearsons," Brooke said.

Seeing the unhappy look on Brooke's face, her German shepherd, Buster, gave her a big kiss on the mouth. "Mom, is it okay if I go for a six-mile run tomorrow morning?"

"I'm always concerned when you run alone."

"I'll take Buster with me. We'll run to school and back along Mulford Road. There's so little traffic there. I'll do it before breakfast. That will give me the rest of the day to go shopping with you."

"Shopping?"

"Yeah, so I can point out some of the cute things I'd love to wear. My birthday is next month. Or have you forgotten?"

"I was in labor for eighteen hours with you. How could I ever forget your birthday?"

The next morning, a chilly but clear day, the first rays of the sun were spreading out across the valley as Brooke and Buster stepped outside. She figured she would be back within an hour, factoring in time for Buster to chase after squirrels and cats and other critters.

Wearing a Mountaineers sweatshirt, shorts, gloves, and a baseball cap sprouting her ponytail, Brooke trotted out of the neighborhood, her dog by her side. She was startled when two oncoming squad cars, their lights flashing but their sirens silent, sped past them. "I wonder where they're going," she said to Buster. She looked behind her. "Wow. They turned into our neighborhood." She kept on running and twice within the first mile had to scold Buster for chasing after squirrels.

Moments later, she jogged past the accident scene from the day before. The fresh ruts from the tires of Mrs. Shearson's car led to a section of the fence that was still lying down in front of the transmission tower. A hubcap lay partially hidden in the grass about 20 feet away. *It's probably from Mrs. Shearson's car,* Brooke thought. *I'll pick it up on the way back.*

Brooke kept on running until she realized that Buster wasn't with her. She turned around and saw that he was sniffing at the base of the tower. "Buster! Get away from there. That's dangerous."

But Buster didn't leave. Instead he looked up at the tower and barked.

"Buster! Come on, boy! Get over here! We're not done running."

The dog whined and barked again, his eyes still locked on something high in the tower. When Buster refused to leave, Brooke was miffed. "Why are you being such a bad boy?" She marched over to the tower. "If you ran a squirrel or a cat up that thing, I'm going to be angry at you."

Buster continued barking and whining, and kept his attention focused high on the tower.

"What is so important up there that you won't listen to me?" She looked up in the morning light but didn't see anything at first, because the early sun was in her eyes. She moved into a shadow and stared. She blinked. And blinked again. "There's a person up there!"

Brooke angled to her left for a better look. It was obvious the person wasn't a electrical lineman. It appeared to be a child sitting on a horizontal beam, known as a cross arm, about 40 feet above the ground. And then it dawned on Brooke: "Oh, my God, it's Corey!"

The boy looked down but said nothing. He swung his legs back and forth.

What should I do? Brooke wondered. *If I run for help, he might fall in the meantime. If I yell at him to come down, he might get scared and fall. And those power lines. If he touches them, he will be electrocuted. What am I going to do?*

As she tried to figure out her course of action, she found herself moving closer to the tower. Brooke knew what had to be done. She just wasn't too keen on scaling a 40-foot-tall tower — especially one that held high-voltage electrical lines. She needed to work up the courage first. But time was short.

She gazed at Corey, who was motioning for her to leave. "Go away!" he shouted. Then he started to stand up.

"Oh, Corey! No! Stay still! Please stay still!" she yelled.

If only someone would drive by right now, they could go get help. She looked up and down the road, but no vehicles were coming from either direction.

Buster barked, a high-pitched yelp this time. Brooke looked up just in time to see Corey's hand come in contact with one of the uninsulated wires — one that carried more than forty-four thousand volts of electricity.

"Corey!" Brooke screamed.

When his hand hit the wire, it triggered a boom followed by a shower of sparks. Corey toppled backward and lost his footing. He rolled off the horizontal beam, but he was saved from a fatal fall when his left leg became snagged between two crisscrossed steel braces under the beam. The unconscious boy dangled upside down, slowly swaying on one leg while his shirt began to smolder.

Without further hesitation, Brooke ran past the DANGER! HIGH VOLTAGE sign and began climbing the tower's ladder. Her heart was pounding wildly as she scrambled higher and higher. *He can't be dead. Oh, please not that.*

As she continued her climb, she tried to remember everything she had learned in science class about electricity. She knew

103

electricity tries to find the path of least resistance to the ground by way of a conductor such as a wire. The human body is also a conductor, and by touching both the ground (or something that is on the ground) and a high-voltage cable simultaneously, it can cause a severe electrical shock.

Brooke also knew that her sneakers and gloves could help block the path of electricity, but if the voltage was high enough, they wouldn't protect her. *Just don't touch any wires,* she told herself. *But what if Corey is energized? What if he's still in contact with a wire?*

She kept climbing, ignoring the growing distance between her and the ground. When she finally reached the horizontal beam where Corey was hanging, she shouted, "Corey! Can you hear me?" There was no response. His shirt was still smoking.

The beam was about eight inches wide but Brooke was too afraid to walk on it, so she straddled it, making sure her head didn't touch the live transmission line above her. She scooted out onto the beam until she reached Corey. With one hand holding on to the beam, she leaned over and beat the smoldering shirt with her glove. *Lucky for him I have really long arms,* she thought.

Suddenly, his limp body jerked. Corey began crying and flailing.

"Corey, please, please, please stay still! I'm trying to help you."

The panic-stricken boy was shrieking now, although Brooke didn't know if it was from fear or from pain. It didn't matter. She had to act fast before he worked himself free and plunged to his death. His leg began slipping out from between the crisscrossed bars. Now the only thing keeping him from falling was his left foot, which was wedged between the bars.

While she straddled the beam and locked her feet underneath her, Brooke reached down and with all her strength, tried to pull Corey up by the waistband of his pants. But she nearly lost her balance, and she screamed in fright. The boy was still wiggling and crying, making Brooke's dangerous rescue effort even more difficult. "Stop it, Corey!" she yelled in exasperation. "I'm trying to help you!"

Clutching the beam with one hand, she leaned over again until her fingers grasped his waistband again. Her arm shaking and burning from the strain, she began lifting him toward her. She shifted her weight to the other side of the beam and finally yanked him onto her lap. Then she freed his left foot.

Still straddling the beam, Brooke held Corey tight. "I've got you. You're going to be safe." She wept with relief.

But then she wondered, *How in the world am I going to get him down?*

Before she could think of a plan, Corey became agitated again and tried to break her hold on him. "Corey, no!" she pleaded. "Don't do that! You'll kill both of us!"

She tried restraining him by pinning his arms, but nearly lost her balance again. She knew her best chance to save him was moving him off the beam and to the main framework of the tower.

But Corey was being difficult. "Go away!" he demanded. "Go away!"

"I can't and I won't. Corey, I'm going to save you whether you like it or not!" *I'm just not sure how. I wish someone would drive by and help us get down.*

Throughout the rescue attempt, Buster kept up a continuous round of high-pitched barks. Hearing her dog, Brooke shouted down, "Buster, go get help!"

Buster backed away from the tower but then returned to the base, unwilling to leave his mistress alone.

"Buster, go get help!"

While giving orders to her dog, Brooke took her eyes off Corey and didn't see his swinging fist until it was too late. He had turned around and socked her square across the jaw. The stunned girl needed to grasp both hands on the beam between her legs to keep from falling off. But now she was totally defenseless and suffered another blow, this time to her nose.

Seeing stars from the impact, Brooke reeled backward. Then she grabbed one of Corey's arms and began dragging him with her as she scooted toward the main framework. Blood was streaming from her nose. "Corey, you're coming with me!"

"Go away!"

"No!" Brooke whipped off her warm-up jacket and wrapped its sleeves around Corey and pinned his arms to his side. "There! Now, try to relax." She wiggled back an inch at a time, pulling the protesting boy with her until they had reached the main framework where the beam was wide enough for both of them. She stood him up, keeping him between a vertical brace and her body.

I can't possibly get him down from here alone, she thought, wiping the blood from her nose. *What am I going to do?*

She looked down and, for the first time since the ordeal began, felt a surge of hope. Buster was barking in the middle of the road as a car approached. The car honked and slowed down, but didn't stop. Instead, it swerved to avoid hitting the dog and kept on going. Brooke's heart sank. *Isn't anyone going to stop and help us?*

A few more minutes crept by. Corey was getting agitated again, trying to squirm free from Brooke's grasp. But she held him firm. When another car came down the road, Buster barked and ran in circles, forcing it to stop. An elderly farmer in bib overalls stepped out. Buster barked some more and then dashed toward the tower, ran back to the farmer and toward the tower again. The farmer understood and followed the dog past the smashed-down fence to the base of the tower.

"Help!" Brooke screamed. "Help! I'm up here!"

The farmer looked up. "What in tarnation are y'all doin' up there?"

"It's a long story," Brooke replied. "Just get help, please. I have a mentally challenged boy up here with me. Call the fire department. Hurry!"

The farmer hustled to his car and squealed off. Corey kept wriggling, trying to get free, but said nothing. "You're not going anywhere until the firemen get here," she told him. Minutes later, when she heard sirens growing louder, tears of relief trickled down her cheeks. *It'll all be over soon,* she told herself, still keeping a tight hold on the boy.

Suddenly, the base of the tower was bursting with activity. Fire engines, squad cars, and emergency vehicles had roared to the scene. Firefighters climbed the tower, secured Corey in a special sling, and gently lowered him to the ground where his parents and an ambulance were waiting for him. He was then rushed to the hospital for treatment of burns to his arms and legs.

The firefighters then put Brooke in the sling and lowered her. As soon as her feet touched the ground, Buster raced over to her and covered her face in kisses. "You did great, Buster," she gushed, hugging him. "You are my hero."

"No, young lady," said one of the firefighters. "*You* are the hero."

When Brooke looked up at the tower and realized what she had done, her body began to shake. Her mind went numb and she burst into sobs. Firefighters wrapped her in a blanket and took her and Buster home.

Brooke later learned that Corey had run away from home early that morning because he was still upset over the accident he had caused. That's why he had climbed the tower. The squad cars that Brooke had seen at the beginning of her run were heading to Corey's house in response to the Shearsons' frantic call after they realized he was missing. Police were setting up a search party to comb the area when the farmer called, saying Corey was on the tower with Brooke.

Corey recovered from his burns, but because he was getting more difficult to handle, his parents felt it was best that he live in a special facility. The day he was scheduled to leave, Brooke stopped by his house to wish him well. But seeing her apparently brought back the bad memory of his scary ordeal on the tower and he began crying.

"I'm sorry," Mrs. Shearson told Brooke. "You saved our boy's life while risking your own life. I wish he understood what your bravery meant to him — and to us."

Brooke started to leave when she felt two small bandaged arms wrap around her waist.

Mrs. Shearson smiled and said, "Oh, isn't that wonderful? He really *does* understand."

THE DESPERATE RACE

"Hee-ya!" Nick Redmond shouted, tugging hard left on the reins of a quarter horse named Blondie. The steed responded instantly and turned sharply around the lone yucca tree. Galloping a tail-length behind him was another quarter horse, Flash, ridden by Nick's pal Adam Peters.

Adam steered Flash to the inside, and within seconds the two were neck and neck coming down the stretch. After a few swift but gentle kicks and slaps from Nick, Blondie surged ahead and streaked across the finish line by a good length and a half.

"The winner and still champion!" Nick roared, thrusting his arms in triumph. As he brought the horse to a trot, he turned around and grinned at Adam. "Sorry, man. But I don't think you'll ever be able to outrace me no matter who you're riding."

The two 15-year-old cowboys, who lived and worked on a West Texas sheep ranch, had weekly races from the corral out to the yucca tree about 200 hundred yards away and back again.

For six weeks in a row, Nick had won, which meant that Adam had to clean out the stalls for another week.

What made it particularly maddening for Adam was that Nick won by riding Adam's horse, Blondie. Nick had wanted to show that the credit for his previous victories shouldn't all go to Flash, so on his suggestion the boys had switched mounts for this latest contest.

"See? It's not the horse but the horsemanship that wins races," Nick said, taking off his soiled cowboy hat and running his hand through his thick, long, sandy-colored hair.

Adam sighed and leaned back on his saddle. *Maybe Nick is right, but I'm not going to admit it,* he thought. "I'm just as good a horseman as you are, Nick. I'll prove it when we're racing for something a lot bigger than who's going to be shoveling manure."

Adam was true to his word just days later when the stakes couldn't have been greater — because a life was on the line.

Nick and Adam were close friends, although they both had such a competitive streak that they were always looking to outdo each other in various one-on-one contests. Nick usually won, whether it was lassoing, target shooting, or horse racing. They tried wrestling each other for fun, but only once. Although Nick was 15 pounds heavier and two inches taller, Adam fought with tenacity and nearly had Nick pinned. Somehow the match, attended by some of the ranch hands who were whooping and hollering, turned ugly and tempers flared between the two boys. They started throwing punches and had to be separated. Once they cooled off, they shook hands. Because their friendship was strong, they put the fight behind them, although neither ever suggested wrestling the other again.

For Adam, any kind of victory over Nick was reason to rejoice, because the wins didn't happen that often and the defeats were often agonizingly close. Adam's horse would be one second too slow, his aim one bull's-eye short, his lariat one inch wide of the mark.

At least Nick didn't gloat. Oh, sure, he would tease Adam, but it was never mean-spirited; it was always in good fun, which Adam appreciated. Not that there was much Adam could do about it except try harder next time. He couldn't exactly take out his frustrations on the owners' son.

Adam had lost his mother to cancer when he was only 12. Shortly afterward, his father became foreman on the sheep ranch owned by Nick's parents. So Adam moved with his dad into a small cabin on a hill overlooking the main corral.

Like Nick, Adam started working as a ranch hand and learned how to tend and care for Rambouillets (pronounced ram-boo-LAYS), a popular breed in the region and valued for its high-quality wool. Among the largest and strongest of the fine-wool sheep, Rambouillets are also good meat animals. The rams (males) are horned, and the ewes (females) are not.

To his credit, Nick didn't lord over the fact that his parents owned the sheep ranch. He didn't duck out of his work or pawn it off on Adam. Nick wanted, and expected, to be treated like every other ranch hand. That was one of the reasons why Adam admired and looked up to Nick.

Before the beginning of each school year, the boys went out on the range, joining other herders on horseback. On endless acres of scrub, more mesquite than grass, they watched over a woolly tide of about 1,000 sheep as two vigilant sheepdogs helped keep the flock moving. Adam loved camping out under the stars and drinking strong coffee (with lots of sugar) over an open fire in the morning and riding Blondie in the wide-open spaces of West Texas. He felt a certain connectedness with the land whenever he heard the baaing of the sheep and the tinkling of their bells.

He wasn't thrilled with doing sentry duty at night, which meant staying awake from midnight to six in the morning while guarding the sheep with his ranch rifle. The danger from coyotes and mountain lions was always a concern in the dark wilderness. He had never seen a mountain lion, which was fine with him. But a year earlier, a coyote managed to kill one of the sheep on his watch — something that had never happened to Nick.

Each day the herders took the sheep to a new piece of land for fresh grazing. They moved three to four miles a day, the flock looking like a low, drifting cloud over the stark scrubland. In the spring, the sheep were driven back to the home ranch where crews who worked morning until night sheared them. Adam and Nick counted the sheep and applied medicine to wounds of any animal accidentally cut. They also tied each bundle of fleece with twine before they placed it in an eight-by ten-foot bag that, when filled, weighed about 360 pounds.

The boys' job also included docking — cutting off all but two inches of the tail — which was done for sanitary and reproductive reasons. They used a special paint to mark the freshly shorn sheep for identification, and they earmarked the animals by notching one or both ears with distinctive combinations of cuts and slashes known as lance points. By using a slightly different mark each year, a rancher could tell the age of his sheep.

During lambing seasons, when the ewes gave birth, the herders carefully watched over the sheep because the first few weeks were critical to the lambs' survival. Sometimes Nick and Adam had to assist a ewe that was having a difficult birth. Other times, the boys needed to encourage or force an indifferent mother to nurse her offspring.

The young cowboys helped move the main group of ewes away from the ewes who had recently lambed. At the crack of dawn, they guided the flock about a half mile from the ewes that had lambed and let them graze and drink. Only after the lambs were old enough to bond with their mothers were the two groups merged into one flock.

During this time, Adam and Nick rode through the ewes and lambs to check for any animals that had a problem. Adam made an extra special effort to help lost lambs. A ewe would get frantic if she got separated from her new lamb. Adam knew that when a ewe lost track of her baby in the flock, she would go back to the spot where she last saw it. If she couldn't find it, she would run willy-nilly, totally out of her mind. He wondered if the reason he took such great satisfaction in reuniting mama and baby had anything to do with how much he missed his own mother.

One day, the boys, who shared a tent during lambing season, came across a ewe that had given birth to triplets, which wasn't uncommon. The problem was that a ewe tends to nurse only two lambs during a season. As a result, one of the lambs needed to be taken away and bottle-fed. There were times when Nick's mother and a helper in a barn had as many as 50 lambs to bottle-feed.

"Should we take the smallest lamb because it's the weakest?" Adam asked Nick.

"Let's take the largest," Nick replied. "Make it easier on my mom. She'll be able to bottle-feed for a shorter time with the biggest lamb than the runt."

One late afternoon, the two boys had reached a gully where a couple of sheep had wandered off. "I'll catch the one on the left; you get the one on the right," Nick said. "The first one who brings it back to this spot . . ." he marked a big X with his boot on the dusty ground, "gets the other guy's piece of cake tonight. What do you say?"

"Fine with me," said Adam. If there was one skill on which he prided himself more than any other it was the way he handled a lariat.

On the count of three, they quickly maneuvered their horses into position. Flash stumbled just as Nick was tossing his lasso and missed the sheep. Adam snared his sheep on the first throw. He tied off one end of the rope to the saddle horn and backed up his horse so the sheep, unhappy at being roped, bleated in protest. Slowly the sheep began moving. Then Adam spotted a lamb behind a yucca. He jumped off his horse, picked up the lamb, got back on Blondie, and draped the baby over his lap.

Meanwhile, Nick lassoed his sheep on his second throw. This animal was more willing to cooperate than Adam's was. By the time Adam arrived at the X, he was too late.

"The winner!" Nick shouted with glee.

"Hey, no fair. My ewe had a lamb nearby that I couldn't leave behind."

"That's tough luck. Man, am I going to enjoy dessert tonight. Mmm. Mmm." Nick rubbed his stomach.

In disappointment, Adam slapped his hat against his thigh. "Ah, cake isn't good for you anyway."

He got off his horse and gently put down the baby. Then he untied the mama sheep, which was still bleating and baaing loudly.

Nick had already dismounted and released his sheep. "I hope it's double chocolate cake. I love double chocolate."

Adam wasn't listening to Nick anymore, because he thought he heard an unsettling sound. Blondie heard it, too, and whinnied as she backed up. "What is it, girl?"

Flash neighed. While Nick was jabbering away about the extra portion of tasty dessert he was going to eat, Adam realized the sound he heard was a rattlesnake. He spotted it coiled up beside a rock next to Flash's left hoof.

"Rattler!" Adam yelled.

Flash saw it, too. He reared up and then bolted. At that exact moment, Nick had turned around to face his horse and inadvertently stepped in the loop of his lariat, which was lying on the ground. The rope was still tethered to his saddle. As the steed broke into a run, the loop tightened around Nick's legs.

He could barely blurt out an "oh, no!" before he was jerked to the ground, landing hard on his back. He tried to sit up, but by then Flash was galloping in a panic, dragging Nick behind him. "Whoa, Flash! Whoa!" Nick shouted.

Seeing his buddy getting towed over rocks and sagebrush, Adam leaped onto Blondie and galloped after him. "Faster, Blondie, faster!" Every time he saw Nick's head slam into a rock, Adam winced. *He's going to get bashed to death if I don't stop Flash,* Adam thought. *I'll have to lasso him to stop him.*

Not taking his eyes off Flash, Adam reached down on his saddle for his lariat. *It's not here!* He knew instantly what had happened to it. Startled by the rattler, he had dropped his lariat and forgot to pick it up when he saw Nick getting dragged off.

"C'mon, Blondie!" yelled Adam, digging his heels into the mount's sides. Second by second, Blondie gained on Flash until she was galloping directly to the right of Nick. The cowboy was bloodied and battered and covering his head with his hands and arms. *At least he's still conscious,* Adam thought.

"Hang tough, Nick! I'll stop him!"

The horses were now neck and neck. Adam leaned over as far as he could and extended his arm, trying to grasp Flash's reins. *Just a few more inches and I'll . . . Darn it!* Flash veered off to the left and headed in a different direction. *I've got to catch him!*

"Eee-ya, Blondie! Go faster, girl!"

Once again, Adam and his horse caught up with Flash. *I'll catch him this time,* he told himself. The horses were side by side and stride for stride as he leaned over. Adam stretched out for the reins, but like his first attempt, his fingers were only a few agonizing inches short of reaching their target.

Get closer . . . closer. He was bent over and out of his saddle when his fingernails brushed against Flash's reins. *Almost . . . I can feel them ...* "Ahhh!" Adam had reached so far over that he lost his balance and was sliding off Blondie. To prevent himself from a dangerous fall, he forced his horse to pull up until he could right himself. By the time Adam was back in his saddle, Flash had made a sharp turn to the right. "Whoa, Flash!" he yelled. "Whoa!"

But the horse remained panicky and continued its wild ride towing Nick. Adam refused to give up and made another charge toward Flash. The young cowboy was getting worried because Nick's arms were flopping aimlessly behind his head, which was banging against rocks and bouncing over thorny brush. He looked like a rag doll being shaken by an invisible dog. *I've got to stop Flash before Nick is killed.*

Up ahead was an arroyo — a gully that had been carved deep and wide by a recent flash flood. Water was still coursing through it. *If I don't stop Flash in time, he'll run into the arroyo and Nick could drown. I can't rein in Flash or lasso him. What else can I do?* In a few seconds, he came up with a wild idea.

The thought terrified him because it meant he faced serious injury and possible death if his rescue plan wasn't executed perfectly. But he was out of options. He had to do it. Adam had decided that his only hope was to leap off Blondie and onto Flash with both steeds at full gallop. *If I miss ... No, I can't miss. I just can't.*

The horses were hurtling ever closer to the arroyo. Eighty yards away ... His mount was now running side by side with Flash ... Seventy yards ... "Eee-ya, Blondie! Eee-ya!" Sixty yards ... Sweat poured down Adam's arms and neck, and his heart pounded wildly. Fifty yards ... Blondie pulled ahead of

Flash by a few feet . . . Forty yards . . . Adam rose from his saddle and moved his feet so only the toes of his boots were in the stirrups. *It's now or never.* Taking a deep breath, Adam leaped off his sprinting horse and flew four feet in the air and onto the right side of Flash's neck . . . Thirty yards . . .

Flash neighed and slowed just a bit from the sudden weight. His dangling legs brushing against the scrubs, Adam wrapped his arms around the horse's foaming neck. But he didn't have a strong grip. *I'm slipping away!* Twenty yards . . . He was now eyeball-to-eyeball with Flash. "Whoa, boy! Whoa!" As Adam started to fall, he clutched on to the bit in the horse's mouth and pulled Flash's head straight down.

Ten yards from the arroyo, Flash slowed to a stop. Adam released his grip and took hold of the rope that was still tied to the saddle horn. Then he followed the rope to his unconscious, bleeding friend.

Dropping to his knees, Adam cradled Nick in his arms and shouted, "Nick! Talk to me!" There was no response. "At least you're breathing." Adam freed Nick's legs from the lariat and then ran to the stream where he soaked his bandanna and filled his canteen. He dashed back and dabbed Nick's cut-and-bruised face with the wet bandanna.

"Come on, Nick. Say something."

Several minutes later, Nick began to moan. Not knowing what else to do, Adam poured water on Nick's head. Nick coughed and opened his eyes. He squinted and winced. "My head . . . my back . . . my arms," he mumbled.

When Nick finally was able to sit up, Adam cringed. Nick's shirt was shredded in the back and his exposed back was crisscrossed with deep cuts. Still dazed and in pain, Nick muttered, "I feel like I've just been dragged across West Texas."

"You were, good buddy."

After cleaning his wounds as best he could in the stream, Nick was helped onto Flash. The injured cowboy remained slumped over for the slow ride back to the ranch. When the boys arrived, Nick's parents drove him 30 miles to the nearest hospital, where he spent the night. He had suffered numerous bruises, lacerations, and a concussion, but incredibly he had no broken bones.

When he returned home the next day, he limped over to Adam and shook his hand. "Thanks, man. You saved my life."

"Don't mention it," said Adam.

"Okay, I won't ever again," Nick replied with a grin and a wink. "Oh, and about your portion of the cake that I won yesterday . . ."

"Don't worry about it. Since you weren't around, I went ahead and ate your slice." Smacking his lips, Adam added, "Double chocolate. It was dee-licious."

THE WHITE DEATH

Danny **Peters gulped.** He could feel the adrenaline surging through his veins. *I'm going too fast,* he told himself. *Ah, heck, no sense slowing down now. Go for it!*

He continued to charge down the unforgiving New Hampshire mountain, his skis carving large S-shaped patterns in the snow in one high-speed turn after another. *Oh, what a rush! What a run! Wow. It doesn't get any better than this.*

Then disaster struck. In a split second, the 17-year-old skier went from exhilaration to despair. His left ski dug in too deep, hit a rock, and snapped in two like a splintered Popsicle stick. Danny cartwheeled in the air and then slammed hard into the snow, knocking off his other ski. Spinning on his stomach, Danny skimmed down the steep slope of Tuckerman Ravine. Snow sprayed up around him as he dug in his ski boots and poles trying to put the brakes on his out-of-control slide. Finally, about fifty yards after the slope flattened out, he skidded to a stop a few feet away from a large boulder.

Danny lay prone in the snow for several seconds, catching his breath and waiting for his body's central nervous system to send pain signals to the brain. When he didn't feel any serious stinging or soreness, he cautiously sat up and moved his arms and legs. *Hey, nothing's broken. Nothing's twisted.* He wiped the snow from his face and goggles and stood up. He turned and waved to three hikers in a nearby gully. They had watched his wipeout with frightened fascination. The grinning teen waved and yelled, "I'm okay!"

"Woo-hoo! Wow! All right!" the hikers shouted. The trio, all college-age guys, clapped in relief.

It was a close call for Danny, but the powerfully built jock had come through without a scratch. "The mountain tried, but it couldn't get me this time," he told them. The hikers gave him a thumbs-up and then moved on up the gully.

He would see them again soon — when they all faced an extreme encounter with The White Death.

The high-school junior from upstate New York was visiting his 18-year-old cousin, Wyatt, in Keene, New Hampshire, in early spring to ski the Tuckerman Ravine. The thousand-foot-high glacial cirque (a ravine shaped like a bowl cut in half) is nestled below the nearby 6,288-foot peak of Mount Washington, known for having the world's worst weather. In 1934, it set the record for the highest recorded wind gust ever — 231 miles per hour. Hurricane-force winds blast its peak an average of 110 days a year. The mountain shudders often from avalanches and falling chunks of ice the size of couches. Adding to the dangers are sharp-edged rocks, crevasses, sudden drops in temperature, and fierce hit-and-run storms. More than 130 people have died on its slopes since the mid-1800s.

Wyatt, a high-school wrestler who had skied Tuckerman's dips, gullies, and chutes several times before, told Danny, "Tuckerman is tough. There are no chairlifts, no paid ski patrols. If you get hurt on the downhill, fall into a crevasse, or get hit by a chunk of falling ice, you're pretty much on your own, because it will be a long time before help arrives."

To Danny, an athletic high-school junior and experienced skier, Tuckerman represented a mental and physical challenge that he looked forward to facing. He might have felt differently had he known he would soon be testing not only his skiing abilities but his survival skills, as well.

On a blustery, bone-chilling Monday morning that would have been better spent at home in front of a crackling fire, Danny and Wyatt drove to the base of Mount Washington. The U.S. Forest Service had posted a warning that said there was a "moderate risk" of avalanches, the second-lowest ranking in its five-point rating system. "Natural avalanches are unlikely today but human-triggered avalanches are possible on steep snow, covered open slopes, and gullies," the bulletin said.

As in all its avalanche warnings, the Forest Service bulletin ended with this: "Visitors to the Ravine should never come expecting to be rescued when something bad happens. Don't rely on other people being around to help you; ultimately your party may be the only rescue team available to respond."

Wyatt told Danny, "A 'moderate risk' means the odds are in our favor. You still want to ski here today?"

"Let's go for it," said Danny eagerly.

To get to the Ravine, the boys carried their ski gear and backpacks on a three-mile uphill hike through the snow-packed backcountry. Once they reached the base of the Ravine, they still faced a difficult climb up an incredibly steep and slippery 800-foot-high slope to the top. They left their backpacks behind a pile of rocks. Holding a ski in each hand and letting their poles dangle by the straps around their wrists, Danny and Wyatt began their slow, grueling ascent. The higher they went, the steeper it became. An hour later, they reached the top and rested at the ridge-line boulder field.

Because it was a weekday and the weather was foul, there weren't many skiers on the mountain, and only a few hardy hikers on one of the nearby rocky gullies.

"People tell me I'm crazy," Wyatt told Danny. "I am. You've got to be nuts to spend hours hiking three miles and then climbing this steep slope in the middle of nowhere just for a chance to scare yourself silly zooming straight down in what is nothing more than a free fall. You'll see for yourself."

The wind was brisk and it began to snow as the two skiers clicked on their skis and moved to the edge.

"Remember to lean forward," Wyatt said. "If you lean back, you'll lose your balance and end up a human snowball."

Butterflies swirled inside Danny's stomach as he peered over the edge. He had never skied on such a terrifyingly steep slope before. "Cool," he said, not wanting to show how nervous he was. *My gosh, the drop is more severe than I thought,* he told himself. "See you down at the bottom . . . alive, I hope."

"I'll be waiting," said Wyatt. Then he yelled, "Geronimo!" and flew off the edge.

Danny shoved his wiry black hair under his red stocking cap, stalling for time. *Just go!* He knew that if he waited much longer, he would psych himself out. *Three . . . two . . . one . . . Go!*

When Danny pushed off, he felt like he had jumped from a high dive because the drop was so extreme. But his skis landed just right on the firm snow and he was on his way down, faster and faster. His turns were sharp and his ski edges held fast. *Weight centered. Speed a little too fast but under control.* Whatever fear he felt had whooshed by him. He was in another world of wind and speed and a blur of white. Every nerve ending tingled with excitement, a skiing thrill he had never experienced before.

About three-quarters of the way down, just when he was sure this was the run of a lifetime, Danny wiped out.

After collecting his remaining ski, he glissaded (descended in a controlled slide on his rear) the rest of the way to the base of the Ravine where Wyatt, who had skied flawlessly, was waiting for him.

"What happened?" asked Wyatt.

"Well, it was an awesome run until I crashed and burned. Snapped a ski, too."

Wyatt shook his head in consolation. "I'm sorry that you ate it big-time, cousin."

"That's okay. Up until then it was mind-boggling. Stupendous. Crazy."

"Say, uh, do you mind if I do another run? It will take only an hour. I mean, we've come all this way and . . ."

"Yeah, sure. Go ahead. I'll just hunker down by our backpacks."

The temperature had been in the low teens, but when the brisk winds kicked up even more, the air quickly plunged to the single digits. Danny tried to stay warm by drinking a thermos of hot chocolate that was barely lukewarm from the bitter cold. He watched Wyatt climb up the Ravine until he lost sight of him in the falling snow. Danny then focused on an icy, steep gully where the three hikers who earlier had applauded his unplanned cartwheel were descending.

The hikers were about two-thirds of the way down when Wyatt completed his second (and again flawless) run. The cousins gathered their gear and headed for the trail that would lead them back to their car. Suddenly, they heard an ominous rumble. They turned around and saw a menacing cloud of snow roaring down the gully directly above the hikers. An unstable mass of snow had broken away from the mountainside and was picking up speed as it rushed downhill.

"Avalanche!" Wyatt shouted. Not knowing how far the dangerous river of snow would surge, Wyatt said, "Hurry, Danny, get behind a boulder. If you're carried away, try to swim with the flow. If you're buried, put your hands in front of your face to create an air pocket."

Hearts pounding in fearful anticipation, they waited for the avalanche — known among skiers as The White Death — to reach them. To their relief, it stopped about 25 yards away, kicking up thick, large curls of snow.

"Whew, that was a lucky break," Wyatt said. "The avalanche didn't get to us."

When the snow cloud cleared, they looked back up. Danny spotted one of the hikers buried up to his waist and struggling to get out of the snow mass's grip. Danny couldn't see the other two anywhere in the wind-whipped snow.

"Come on, Wyatt, we have to help him!"

After grabbing their ski poles, they slogged in the knee-deep snow to the first hiker, who had managed to free himself by the time they arrived. Holding a handful of snow over a gash on his forehead, he kept weaving in circles.

"My buddies! I can't find them! I think they're buried!"

"Where did you last see them?" asked Wyatt.

"Farther up the gully," replied the hiker, who said his name was Stan Monroe.

"Could they have gotten out of the way?" asked Danny.

"It's unlikely," Stan replied. "The avalanche hit us so fast, we didn't even realize what was happening until it was too late. They could be anywhere. Steven Lipinski is wearing a red jacket and Mike Gordon is wearing a blue one."

"Was there anyone else hiking in the gully?" Danny asked.

"I don't think so."

For a brief moment, the wind blew an opening in the steadily falling flakes long enough for Danny to spot what looked like a bright red sleeve sticking out of the snow about 100 yards up the gully. "I think I see Steven." About 50 yards from that point, Danny also noticed someone in blue lying motionless on any icy 15-foot-high ledge.

Below, Danny and the other two heard a terrible rumble again. Another avalanche, a smaller one, poured down a narrow chute that crossed the gully not far from where Steven was buried. "We've got to get up there and see if those guys are alive," said Danny.

Wyatt turned to Stan. "Do you feel strong enough to hike to the ski-patrol cabin about a mile down the trail and call for help?"

Stan, still holding his head, nodded. "Yeah, I can do that."

"Good. Danny, let's go help those other guys."

As they made their way to Steven, the cousins both had the same concern: *Will there be more avalanches today?*

It was hard going up the snow-packed gully. "We've got no more than fifteen minutes to dig him out before he suffocates," Wyatt explained. "When an avalanche stops, the snow can set as hard as cement around its victims."

When the teens reached the red sleeve, they began digging around it.

"Steven, we're going to get you out!" Wyatt shouted. "Wiggle your fingers if you can hear us."

The index finger poking out of the sleeve of the red jacket moved back and forth.

"He's alive!" Danny shouted.

Using their hands and ski poles, the cousins dug furiously until they uncovered Steven's head. In a stroke of luck, he had managed to create an air pocket before the snow had set, so he was able to breathe — but barely — until they cleared out a bigger area. He groaned and gulped for air.

"Thank God," Steven gasped. "I thought I was dying. So hard to breathe." He grimaced and clutched the arm that had been sticking out from under the snow. "It hurts. It's broken for sure."

When they had removed snow from around his waist, they

128

tried to pull him out but he wouldn't budge. It was as if he was glued to the snow. Another five minutes of burrowing was needed to free him.

"Stay here with Steven," Wyatt told Danny. "I'll check on the other guy."

"No, let me do it," said Danny. "I'm taller than you and a better climber."

"Evens and odds. I'll start the count with you first. Winner goes." On the count of three, they each held up fingers — Danny, two; Wyatt, three. "Okay, Danny," said Wyatt. "Go, but be careful. That's not an easy climb without an ice axe."

While Wyatt helped Steven off the gully, Danny headed up toward the ledge. The wind had shifted and was now blowing at about 60 miles an hour. The snow was coming down so heavily that he could see only 20 feet ahead. At the base of the ledge, Danny looked for toeholds and carefully began his climb. About five feet up, he slid back down. Again and again, he tried and failed. So he took a different route, a longer one on the far side of the gully that eventually brought him above the ledge. He could see the hiker lying prone, facedown.

"Hello down there!" he shouted. "Are you hurt? Are you Mike Gordon?"

The young man turned onto his side and, grimacing in pain, blurted, "Yes to both questions. I need help!"

Danny faced a drop of about five feet onto the narrow ledge. If he missed, he would tumble another 15 feet. He eased his body over the edge and tried to climb down, but it was too icy and he lost his grip. He landed hard right next to Mike's head.

"It's unbelievable," Mike said. "The avalanche picked me up

and carried me down the gully and then left me here on this ledge. I'm pretty sure I broke my leg. I can't move."

Danny looked at Mike's leg, which was bent at a weird angle. Blood was seeping through his pants. Danny could tell it was the worst kind of break — a compound fracture, when the bone protrudes through the skin.

"What about Steven and Stan?" Mike asked. "Did they survive?"

"Yeah, they're both alive. Steven was buried but we got him out. He has a broken arm. And Stan seems okay, although his head was bleeding. He went to get help."

Mike started shivering. "Man, it's freezing cold. I want to get off of this rock."

"Okay, stay calm," said Danny. "Help should be coming shortly."

"You won't leave me, will you?"

"No. I'll stay until mountain rescue gets here."

The bleeding had stopped, but the broken leg needed to be put in a splint. Using his ski pole, Danny placed it against the leg and then secured it with a handkerchief.

The temperature was plunging and the storm was cranking up. Darkness was settling in. *Where is the rescue team?* Danny wondered. *Why hasn't help arrived?*

Trying to take Mike's mind — as well as his own — off of their grim situation, Danny asked him questions. He learned that Mike, Stan, and Steven were roommates at the University of Massachusetts looking to experience a challenging winter hike. "We got more than we bargained for," said Mike, a short, lean 20-year-old.

The two talked about college life — sports, fraternities, and, most important, girls. "Man, there are some good-looking girls at U. Mass," Mike said. "We have parties every weekend. You have to come for a visit. You'll have a blast."

"Sounds great," said Danny, wishing he were at a party right now.

Talking helped distract Mike from the pain, but only for a little while. They were now caught in a major blizzard. Every minute that passed only made Danny worry more. The shrieking wind and the heavy snow made it impossible for him to communicate with Wyatt. He knew that rescuers — wherever they were — would never be able to find them under these horrible conditions.

There was a reason why a rescue team hadn't arrived. Earlier, while Danny was trying to reach Mike, Wyatt had led Steven to a natural shelter under a narrow space between two large boulders at the base of the Ravine. About a half hour later, Wyatt spotted Stan staggering in the deep snow on the trail. "Stan, where's the rescue team? When will they get here?"

"Rescue team?" mumbled Stan, streaks of blood frozen on his face. "What's going on? Where am I?"

"You're at Tuckerman Ravine. The avalanche. You went to get help, remember?" Seeing the blank stare in Stan's eyes, Wyatt's heart sank. *Oh, great. He's probably got a concussion and has been wandering around without ever getting help.* He took Stan by the hand and guided him to where Steven was huddling. "You two stay here. I'll go get help. Whatever you do, don't move!"

Wyatt looked up the gully, trying to spot Danny and Mike.

But in the snowy dusk it was impossible to see them. *I hope they're all right. It's going to be a long night for them. For all of us.* Wyatt plodded through the snow, now waist-deep, and bitter cold, knowing that it would take him nearly an hour just to reach a phone. *There will be no rescue tonight.*

Back on the ledge, Mike was starting to drift in and out of consciousness. His body was quivering from the cold. So was Danny's. Adding to their miseries, chunks of ice from ledges higher up were crashing around them. Above the din of the raging storm, Danny thought he heard thunder. *Another avalanche.*

"Mike, we have to move."

"I can't. I'm in too much pain."

"If we can move about twenty feet to our right on this ledge, we can get behind an outcropping. It will help protect us from an avalanche and act as a break against the wind. Just scoot on your rear. Come on."

Danny got behind Mike, grabbed him under the arms, and began pulling him. Mike screamed out in pain with each movement, but eventually they were able to get on the other side of the rock.

"They're not coming are they?" Mike said. "We're going to freeze to death on this ledge."

"No way," Danny declared. "They'll be here. Any minute now." *Where are they? Why aren't they here?*

The wind would not stop howling. And the cold kept getting colder. Danny had pressed Mike against the wall and lay across his upper body, trying to keep him warm and block out the wind and snow.

For the first time since the ordeal unfolded, Danny was

wondering if there would even be a rescue. *If they show up at the Ravine, how are they going to find us? Nobody can see at night in this blizzard. We're going to have to ride it out.*

"I'm cold and hungry and hurting," Mike muttered.

Danny remembered he had a Baby Ruth candy bar that he had put between his T-shirt and flannel shirt above his belt so that his body heat would keep it from freezing. He quickly opened his jacket, vest, and shirt and pulled out the candy bar. "Hey, we're in luck. I brought dinner."

His hands were trembling from the cold as he snapped the Baby Ruth into four pieces. He gave two to Mike. "This is the appetizer. Your main course is the other piece. Keep it tucked inside your jacket before it freezes."

When they consumed the candy, Danny scooped up a handful of snow and put it to Mike's lips. "You need to stay hydrated. Let this snow melt in your mouth." Like Mike, Danny swallowed several scoops of snow.

"I don't know if I can make it through the night," Mike shuddered. "It's too cold."

"We'll get through this. I promise."

Danny rubbed Mike's arms and body, trying to keep the circulation moving. He also rubbed Mike's good leg.

During the night, Danny thought he saw some fuzzy lights below in the blizzard. *The rescue team? Could it be them?* "Hey, over here! Over here!" He shouted at the top of his lungs, but in the fierce wind there was no way they could hear him. He wanted to climb down in the blinding snow and darkness. He nixed the idea, knowing it would be too dangerous. Besides, he promised he wouldn't leave Mike. *We just have to tough it out until morning. I hope he makes it through the night. Heck, I hope I do.*

He curled up next to Mike and fell asleep. At first light, Danny woke up covered in snow. His body ached all over, and his muscles complained every time he moved. But he heard something that made him smile — nothing. No screaming wind. No falling ice. *It's stopped snowing! The storm is over!* He immediately checked on Mike. His breathing was slow and shallow. He was sleeping — or unconscious; Danny couldn't tell.

He looked down at the bottom of the gulley. His spirits soared even more. He saw several tents at the base of the Ravine. *The rescue team!* "Hey!" he yelled. "Hey! Hey! We're up here on the ledge!"

One head popped out of the tent. Then another and another. Members of the rescue team had arrived late the previous evening after Wyatt's valiant hike in the blizzard to get help. By the time the team reached Tuckerman, the visibility and treacherous conditions made it impossible to search for Mike and Danny. The team was able to treat Steven and Stan and get them safely out of the Ravine.

The remaining members spent the night in tents, waiting for daylight before launching a rescue attempt. Wyatt, refusing to go home, stayed with them.

At daybreak, the rescuers assembled their gear and headed toward the ledge. It was extremely difficult because of the snow and ice, but, with ropes and a stretcher, they soon lowered Mike off the perch. He was suffering from shock, frostbite, and a compound fracture. Danny slid down a rope and was embraced by his cousin.

"Hey, you wanted an adventure," Wyatt told Danny.

"The next time we ski together, let's do it in the summer — on a lake."

Danny, who was showing symptoms of hypothermia, was wrapped in a special blanket. Weary, achy, and shivering, he had remained on the ledge with the injured hiker for 17 harsh hours.

As Mike was being carried out of Tuckerman, he grabbed Danny's hand and squeezed it. "Thanks, man. You saved my life."

"Hey, I couldn't let you die up there," said Danny. "I need you to introduce me to all those cute girls you promised I'd meet."

About the Author

Allan Zullo is the author of nearly 90 nonfiction books on subjects ranging from sports and the supernatural to history and animals.

He has written the best-selling Haunted Kids series, published by Scholastic, which are filled with chilling stories based on, or inspired by, documented cases from the files of ghost hunters. Allan also has introduced Scholastic readers to the Ten True Tales series, about kids who have met the challenges of dangerous, sometimes life-threatening, situations. In addition, he has authored two books about the real-life experiences of kids during the Holocaust—*Survivors: True Stories of Children in the Holocaust* and *Heroes of the Holocaust: True Stories of Rescues by Teens.*

Allan, the grandfather of two boys and the father of two grown daughters, lives with his wife Kathryn on the side of a mountain near Asheville, North Carolina. To learn more about the author, visit his Web site at www.allanzullo.com.